OSPREY AIRCRAFT OF THE

Ki-27 'Nate'

SERIES EDITOR: TONY HOLMES

OSPREY AIRCRAFT OF THE ACES 103

Ki-27 'Nate' Aces

Nicholas Millman

OSPREY
PUBLISHING

Front Cover

Nomonhan, June 1939. With the conflict raging between Japan and the USSR over the disputed border region of Manchuria and Mongolia, on the afternoon of 22 June formations of Japanese and Soviet fighters clashed in sweeping aerial battles between Bain-Tsagan hill and Lake Buyr Nuur. Sgt Maj Shogo Saito, the most successful pilot of the 24th Sentai over Nomonhan with more than 26 victories claimed, had claimed four I-16s during dogfights that day – including one where the pilot bailed out immediately upon being attacked. He then strafed Soviet aircraft on the ground – an act of aggression that nearly ended his career when he found himself out of ammunition and boxed in by two flights of I-16s that were determined to force him down over Mongolian territory.

Choosing his moment, Saito suddenly lifted the nose of his Ki-27 and turned sharply into one of the Soviet fighters, heading straight for it. His opponent tried to dive beneath Saito's Ki-27, but the fin of his I-16 collided with the Japanese pilot's starboard tailplane. The stricken Polikarpov fell away out of control as the others scattered in confusion. Saito managed to regain control of his damaged aircraft and escape back to his home airfield. His Ki-27, the many bullet holes marked by arrows, was later put on display in Tokyo (*Cover artwork by Ronnie Olsthoorn*)

Dedication

In memory of all the young men who flew, fought and died for their countries in the years 1937-45.

First published in Great Britain in 2013 by Osprey Publishing
Midland House, West Way, Botley, Oxford, OX2 0PH
43-01 21st Street, Suite 220B, Long Island City, NY, 11101, USA

E-mail: info@ospreypublishing.com

Osprey Publishing is part of the Osprey Group

A CIP catalogue record for this book is available from the British Library

ISBN: 978 1 84908 662 2
PDF e-book ISBN: 978 1 84908 663 9
e-Pub ISBN: 978 1 78096 412 6

Edited by Tony Holmes
Cover Artwork, Aircraft Profiles and Line Art by Ronnie Olsthoorn
Index by Alan Thatcher
Originated by PDQ Digital Media Solutions, UK
Printed in China through Asia Pacific Offset Limited
13 14 15 16 17 10 9 8 7 6 5 4 3 2 1

Osprey Publishing is supporting the Woodland Trust, the UK's leading woodland conservation charity, by funding the dedication of trees.

www.ospreypublishing.com

ACKNOWLEDGEMENTS
The author gratefully acknowledges the kind assistance of the following contributors – *Arawasi*, P C Boer, Mary-Grace Browning, Richard Dunn, Neil Frances, Ken Glass, Bill Gordon, Mark Haselden, Ryusuke Ishiguro, Dr Yasuho Izawa, James F Lansdale, James I Long, Carl Molesworth, Keishiro Nagao, Ronnie Olsthoorn, Joe Picarella, Luca Ruffato, Henry Sakaida, Summer, William Swain, Osamu Tagaya, Akio Takahashi, Hiroshi Umemoto, Leszek A Wieliczko, Yoshito Yasuda and Edward M Young. Credited photographs reproduced with the kind permission of Summer (http://blog.goo.ne.jp/summer-ochibo).

CONTENTS

INTRODUCTION

The story of the nimble Ki-27 'Nate' fighter in the service of the Dai-Nippon Teikoku Rikugun Kokutai (Imperial Japanese Army Air Force (JAAF)) is perhaps most often associated with the brief but intense period of air combat between Japan and the Soviet Union over Nomonhan in the summer of 1939. Its use as a frontline fighter during the first months of the Pacific War was somewhat overshadowed by the introduction of more modern fighters such as the Ki-43 Hayabusa and Ki-44 Shoki (see Osprey *Aircraft of the Aces 85* and *100*, respectively), and of course by the ubiquity of the more famous Mitsubishi A6M Zero-sen fighter of the Imperial Japanese Navy Air Force (IJNAF), which was reported to be in some places that it never was!

Although the Ki-27 continued to be operated as frontline equipment by many fighter Sentai well into 1943, especially over China, its exploits are obscure. As the JAAF re-equipped with the latest types the Ki-27 found a supplementary role as an operational trainer, becoming the first true fighter that most Army pilots would fly. Towards the end of the war it was also expended as a stop-gap aerial defender against the increasing bombing raids on Japan and as a special attacker in kamikaze (divine wind) suicide attacks against Allied ships.

Nomonhan was the crucible that forged a generation of JAAF fighter pilots, and many of the surviving Ki-27 aces and notable aviators from that conflict furthered their flying – and fighting – careers in other fighter types. This book tells the stories of some of them, whilst at the same time providing an insight to the place of the Ki-27 within the context of the aerial campaigns fought by the JAAF.

The true origin of the Ki-27 lies in the Nakajima Ki-11 fighter design of 1935. This monoplane machine featuring a radial air-cooled engine, wire-braced wings and a fixed spatted undercarriage was similar in

The Nakajima PE private-venture fighter was developed prior to the issuing of the Army Air HQ requirement for an 'advanced fighter'. Completion of this aircraft in July 1936 led to the construction of the essentially similar Ki-27 prototype that would fly in October 1938 (*Picarella Collection*)

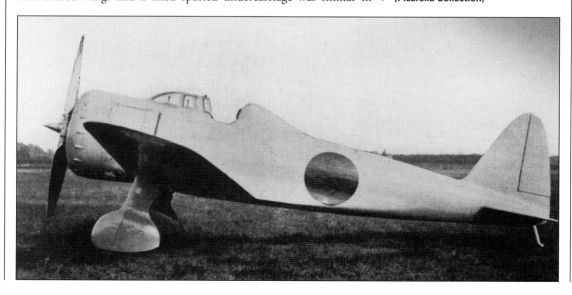

A pair of Type 89 7.7 mm fixed machine guns, with 500 rounds per weapon, formed the armament of the Ki-27 in all models. The guns were fitted to the floor of the cockpit and synchronised to fire through the airscrew between the lower engine cylinders at a rate of 900 rounds per minute and a muzzle velocity of 2690 ft per second. They were fed with disintegrating belt ammunition, the type and combination of which were a matter of unit choice. This weapon, made by the Tokyo, Kokura and Nagoya Army Arsenals, was a revised version of a licence-built Vickers Class E machine gun that was chambered to fire an improved 0.303-in round (7.7 mm x 58 SR). The Japanese Army classified it as a teppou (military rifle, abbreviated as 'te') type kikan juu (machine gun) – e.g. rifle calibre. The 7.7 mm guns were essentially World War 1-vintage armament configuration for a fighter. Any automatic weapon above 11 mm in calibre was classified as a kikan hou or 'machine cannon', regardless of the type of ammunition fired from it (*Picarella Collection*)

appearance to the Boeing P-26 Peashooter pursuit fighter that entered service with the US Army Air Corps in 1934. The Ki-11 was designed to compete in a JAAF competition to select a fighter to replace the rejected Kawasaki Ki-5 design. Rather than an anachronism, wire-bracing was chosen by Nakajima so that it could fit the Ki-11 with a thinner wing in an effort to reduce drag and increase speed. However, the Ki-11 lost out in competition to Kawasaki's Ki-10 metal fuselage biplane, fitted with a liquid-cooled inline engine, because the JAAF favoured manoeuvrability over speed, although the Ki-10 was also found to climb faster.

Despite this failure the Ki-11 gained prestige in civil operation as the AN-1 Communication Aircraft after the last of four prototypes was purchased by a Japanese newspaper, given the registration J-BBHA and used to set a number of speed records. Two of the prototypes remained with Nakajima for the purpose of research, design and development, and they ultimately contributed to the design of a private venture monoplane fighter rolled out in July 1936. Designated PE for 'Pursuit Experimental', this aircraft also featured an air-cooled radial engine and a fixed spatted undercarriage, but benefited from further technological refinement and had cantilever rather than wire-braced wings. It was a remarkably simple, clean and modern looking aircraft.

The imperative for this private venture remains obscure, and some sources assert that it was the result of a tip-off from the Koku Hombu (Air Headquarters of the Imperial Army) regarding the specification requirement for an 'advanced fighter' issued in early 1936. Nakajima was able to commence work on its design early, thus stealing a march on its main competitors Mitsubishi and Kawasaki. This challenging JAAF specification required a high-performance monoplane fighter with sufficient manoeuvrability to compete favourably with traditional biplane designs.

In early 1937 the Nakajima design, now refined even further into an aircraft designated the Ki-27, commenced an exhaustive test programme alongside Mitsubishi and Kawasaki designs at the JAAF Technical Air Research Institute at Tachikawa. By the spring of 1937 the Koku Hombu had decided to order ten pre-production examples of the Ki-27. It had been found during the test programme that Nakajima had struck a clever balance between performance and potential reliability, simplicity, ease of operation and maintenance. Spurred on by this preliminary order, Nakajima tooled up for series production at its Factory No 1 in Ota.

The ten pre-production aircraft were constructed between July and December 1937, and in that same month the Koku Hombu finally approved the Ki-27 for series production as the JAAF's Type 97 Fighter (Kyu-Nana Shiki Sento-ki or Kyu-Nana Sen – 97-Sen, for short).

INTO ACTION OVER CHINA

By March 1938 a total of 32 series production Ki-27s had been manufactured, and on 3 April 1938 the first operational examples were delivered to the 1st Chutai (Squadron) of the 2nd Hiko Daitai (Air Battalion) at Yangchow (now Yangzhou), in central China. At that time the 2nd Hiko Daitai was equipped with the Ki-10 – the biplane fighter that had been ordered in preference to the Ki-11 – and was engaged in supporting the 1st Army campaign against Chinese forces in Shensi Province (now Shaanxi). The squadron was part of the Yamase Unit (commanded by Col Masao Yamase), an ad hoc combat group consisting of a reconnaissance detachment, fighter squadron and two light bomber squadrons from Maj Gen Tadatsugu Chiga's 3rd Hiko Dan (Air Brigade).

In recent fighting against the Chinese, Ki-10 pilot Lt Kosuke Kawahara had achieved *Gekitsui-oh* status (literally 'shoot down king', the approximate equivalent to 'ace' in Japanese), whilst squadron commander Capt Tateo Kato had claimed four victories. The latter would later become leader of the famous 64th Sentai (which incorporated the 2nd Daitai as its 1st and 2nd Chutai), and renowned in Japan as 'Gunshin Kato' (War God Kato), claiming a total of 18 victories before his death in air combat in May 1942 (see *Aircraft of the Aces 13* and *85* for further details). In March 1938 the squadron received a unit citation as recognition for its operational successes over China.

The arrival of the new fighter was well timed as JAAF units had recently begun to experience increasing opposition from Chinese Air Force units re-equipping with new Russian aircraft such as the fast Tupolev SB (*Skorostnoi Bombardirovschik* or high-speed bomber) and Polikarpov I-15bis biplane and I-16 monoplane fighters.

After an uneventful encounter on 9 April, three Ki-27s of the 1st Chutai (flown by Capt Kato, WO Morita and Sgt Maj Saito), together with 12 Ki-10s of the 2nd Daitai Hombu (HQ flight) and the 2nd Chutai, all led by the Daitai commander Maj Tamiya Teranishi, encountered Chinese fighters from the 3rd and 4th Pursuit Groups (PGs). The Chinese force, led by Maj Lin Tsuo, consisted of 11 I-15bis from the 22nd and 23rd Pursuit Squadrons (PSs) of the 4th PG, covered at a higher altitude by seven I-15bis of the 3rd PG. The Chinese fighters were returning to base at Kuei-teh following an attack on Japanese army positions.

Four new Ki-27 Ko fighters of the 1st Chutai, 2nd Hiko Daitai share part of an airfield complex in China with the unit's Kawasaki Ki-10 biplane fighters in June 1938. The curious tented structures are servicing shelters to allow groundcrews to work on engines during the frequent torrential rain (*Yasuho Izawa*)

Maj Tateo Kato, known throughout the JAAF as 'Gunshin Kato' ('War God Kato'), took command of the 64th Sentai in April 1941 after distinguishing himself as a Chutai leader in the 2nd Daitai during 1937-38. Kato was a high-scoring JAAF pilot in operations over China (excluding Nomonhan), with nine victories to his credit, including two claimed in the Ki-27 only seven days after the new type was first delivered, and three scored over Hoizhou in May 1941. By the time of his death in May 1942 whilst flying a Ki-43 in combat against a Blenheim IV bomber of No 60 Sqn RAF over the Bay of Bengal, Kato had claimed 18 victories. The badge on his right breast pocket signifies his command of a Chutai (squadron or company), in this case the 1st Chutai, 2nd Daitai (*Yasuho Izawa*)

The 1st Chutai fighters immediately targeted the lower formation and a classic dogfight began, subsequently described by one of the Chinese pilots as 'pursuers and pursued circling in increasingly tight turns'. Capt Kato and his two wingmen attacked an I-15bis flown by Lt Chang Kuang-ming, who tried to evade with a half-roll followed by a climb, but was hit and lost control of his aircraft. He managed to bail out before the I-15bis caught fire, and although Japanese fighters attempted to strafe him during his parachute descent he landed with just a back injury.

The Ki-27 flight was then attacked by the Chinese top cover. Sgt Maj Risaburo Saito was on the tail of a 23rd PS I-15bis when he came under fire from one of the top cover fighters flown by Zhu Jia-xun – a pilot who would later achieve ace status. Zhu's fire hit the Ki-27, either killing or incapacitating Saito, as the JAAF fighter then veered away sharply and collided with the I-15bis flown by Lt Chen Hui-min. Both fighters tumbled to the ground, but not before Lt Chen was able to bail out with an injured leg. Zhu was in turn attacked by either Capt Kato or WO Morita, who shot away the engine cowling of his I-15bis. He was able to evade them, however, and force land in a wheat field.

A second I-15bis from the 3rd PG subsequently made a forced landing with damage, while a third machine from the group was shot down and its pilot killed. Two Chinese pilots also returned to their airfield with wounds. The 4th PG had had two I-15bis shot down, while three others force landed due to battle damage or fuel starvation. Capt Kato claimed that he had shot down two of the Chinese fighters, as did WO Morita.

The following month Capt Kato returned to Japan with nine victories to his credit. Command of the 1st Chutai duly passed to Capt Mitsugu Sawada, who by that time had four confirmed victories as well as a third-share in a fifth.

The small contingent of Ki-27s were in action again on 20 May when three of the new fighters, together with seven Ki-10s from the 1st Chutai, three aircraft of the Daitai commander's flight and 11 aircraft from the 2nd Chutai, sortied against Lanfeng. They were sent aloft as part of the JAAF's effort to support Japanese Army operations against Chinese troops retreating from Tungshan. The fighters targeted the Chinese airfields at Changan and Hsinyang, around Shangchiu and east of Lanfeng.

Maj Teranishi led both his flight and the 2nd Daitai against a group of four Chinese aircraft, which were soon joined by others, whilst the three Ki-27s pursued two enemy machines. Although unable to catch up with the Chinese fighters, the Nakajima pilots soon spotted ten more aircraft and began stalking them instead, from above and behind. Capt Sawada, leading the Ki-27 flight, accidentally fired his guns prematurely, causing part of the Chinese formation to scatter and dive away. Moments later the Japanese pilots engaged what remained of the Chinese force, with Capt Sawada claiming three fighters shot down and Lt Katsumi Anma and Sgt H Wada one apiece. Lt Anma, flying his first combat sortie, would later become the 64th Sentai's 3rd Chutai leader. He claimed a total of 32 aerial victories before being shot down and killed by P-40s of the American Volunteer Group (AVG) over Loiwing on 8 April 1942.

The 2nd Chutai claimed an additional seven victories, for a total of 12 altogether. The aircraft encountered by the unit were probably I-15bis from the 17th PS and Curtiss Hawk IIIs from the 22nd PS, both part of

The damaged Ki-27 Ko of Capt Mitsugu Sawada, 1st Chutai leader of the 64th Sentai, is examined by staff officers following air combat in China on 8 June 1938. The 64th pioneered the new fighter in action against the Chinese from 9 April 1938 onwards (*Yasuho Izawa*)

Capt Mitsugu Sawada , photographed off-duty in China. In 1932 Sawada had graduated from the Rikugun Koukuu Shikan Gakkō (JAAF Academy) and had already served as a respected fighter instructor at Akeno prior to joining the 2nd Daitai in China in July 1937. On 30 January 1938 he claimed three victories in a day, and on 20 May another hat-trick in one of the unit's first Ki-27s. By the time he was shot down and killed in a Ki-43 over Rabaul on 5 March 1943 whilst serving as the 1st Chutai leader of the 1st Sentai, Sawada had claimed a total of 11 victories (*Yasuho Izawa*)

the 5th PG. Four I-15bis were shot down and two more force landed near Japanese positions, although their pilots managed to evade capture and eventually return to their airfield. Two Hawk IIIs were also shot down and the I-15bis of the 17th PS commander, Cheng Jiu-liu, was damaged.

Mitsugu Sawada was a 27-year-old ex-fighter instructor from the Akeno Flying School who had a reputation for being highly skilled in aerial combat. He had also acquired the rather unfortunate nickname of 'King of the Forced Landing' during his time in China. Keen to take the fight to the enemy whenever possible, on one occasion he had pursued a Chinese reconnaissance type whilst at the controls of an unarmed aircraft, making machine gun noises with his mouth until his opponent was shot down by Lt Kosuke Kawahara!

After a visit to Germany in 1941 and promotion to the rank of major, Mitsugu Sawada was given command of the 1st Sentai, which was then equipped with the Nakajima Ki-43 Hayabusa.

Sawada was killed in action shortly after taking off from Lae, in New Guinea, on 5 March 1943. The undercarriage of his Ki-43 had failed to retract, and witnesses on the ground claimed that despite this handicap he destroyed three American fighters in a desperate 30-minute fight against superior numbers before he was finally downed. These successes took Sawada's victory tally to 11.

Lt Iori (or Iwori) Sakai, flying in the 2nd Chutai on 20 May 1938, also claimed a Chinese fighter shot down during this engagement whilst at the controls of either a Ki-10 or a Ki-27 – sources list both types. This victory was his fifth over China, thus making him an ace. Twenty-nine-year-old Lt Sakai was a former civilian pilot who had graduated from Tokorozawa and served with the JAAF as an NCO reservist for four years, before attending the Army Military Academy in 1932-33 and then instructing at the Akeno Army Flying School. He would see action with the 2nd Chutai throughout the Nomonhan conflict, eventually becoming its leader. Thanks to his background as an instructor, Lt Sakai was able to teach the less experienced pilots in his unit the necessary skills required to successfully employ the Ki-27 in combat.

The 'Sakai Method', drawing on knowledge of enemy air combat tactics, continued to be taught when Lt Sakai returned to Akeno in July 1941. Indeed, it was the basis upon which many future JAAF aces forged their fighting careers.

Capt Iori Sakai (nine victories) was the 64th Sentai's 2nd Chutai leader, and he is seen here with his Ki-27 Otsu at Canton in early 1941. Capt Sakai was instrumental in teaching new pilots combat methods in the Ki-27, and in July 1941 he was posted to Akeno as a flying instructor. After promotion to major in March 1943, he served at the Army Flight Test Centre and flew a Ki-61 Hien in air defence operations against the B-29 raids, claiming one of the bombers shot down. During 1945 Sakai became the chief test pilot for the Ki-100, the radial-engined version of the Ki-61 (*Yasuho Izawa*)

REORGANISATION AND IMPACT

There was a lull in the action in China in late July 1938 following the initial deployment of the Ki-27, and the JAAF took this opportunity to reorganise its structure. The Hiko Daitai (Air Battalions) and Hiko Rentai (Air Regiments) were split up into pure flying elements known as Hiko Sentai thanks to the creation of Airfield Battalions, which were separate ground support units charged with maintenance, supply and airfield security. This organisational structure would provide remarkable flexibility when it came to deploying and moving aircraft to, and within, theatres of operations. The Hiko Dan (Air Brigade), which had previously been just an administrative headquarters, was formally established to have direct command of a combination of reconnaissance, fighter and either light or heavy bomber units of Chutai or Sentai strength.

In August 1938 the 1st and 2nd Chutai of the 2nd Daitai consolidated with the 9th Dokuritsu Hiko Chutai (Independent Air Squadron) to become the three squadrons of the new 64th Hiko Sentai, commanded by Maj Tamiya Teranishi. The Sentai headquarters, together with the 1st and 2nd Chutai, moved to Tientsin and then on to Ertaokou airfield (dubbed 'Nitoko' by the Japanese) near Kiukian, in central China, as part of the 4th Hiko Dan, commanded by Maj Gen Tomo Fujita.

During this period of low aerial activity in September-October 1938, the 2nd Chutai converted wholly to the Ki-27. The 3rd Chutai of the 64th was brigaded with the 27th and 30th light bomber Sentai under the direct command of the North China Area Army Air Group.

Whilst the 64th Sentai was pioneering the Ki-27 in action over China, other Japanese units were being established with the new fighter. In July 1938 the 59th Sentai formed at Kagamigahara, in Japan, with two Chutai from the former 1st Hiko Rentai. It subsequently moved to Manchuria and then on to Ertaokou in November of that year, by which time opportunities for aerial combat had decreased.

July 1938 also saw the formation of the 4th Sentai at Tachiarai, in Japan, with a single Ki-27 Chutai and a reconnaissance Chutai. In August of that same year the 5th Sentai was established with two training Chutai, reorganising in June 1939 following the creation of three fighter Chutai.

Most of these home-based units were initially equipped with a mixture of Ki-10 and Ki-27 fighters, with the latter type increasing in quantity as more became available. In September 1938 the 24th Sentai was established in Manchuria with two Chutai of Ki-27s drawn from the 11th Sentai, which had itself formed only a month earlier. Both of these Manchurian-based Ki-27 units took no part in the fighting over China until after Nomonhan, however.

Personnel of the 59th Sentai in front of one of the unit's Ki-27s at Hankow, China, in late 1939. 1Lt Yasuhiko Kuroe (30 victories), seated second from left in the front row, would forge a notable career with the 64th Sentai over Burma and in other units (see *Aircraft of the Aces 13, 85* and *100*). Standing second left is Sgt Maj Katsutaro Takahashi (nine victories), who would become the 59th's leading Ki-43 ace over Malaya, Sumatra and Java during 1941/42. To his right is Sgt Maj Isamu Kashiide (nine victories), who would become a Bukosho winner and the 4th Sentai's leading ace flying the Ki-45 with seven B-29s claimed (*Yasuho Izawa*)

From July 1938 the 10th Dokuritsu Hiko Chutai (Independent Flying Squadron – DHC) had also converted to the Ki-27. A short while later the unit saw action in the new fighter whilst supporting the advance to Nanking, after which it moved to Anking (now Anqing) in August, to Hankow in November and finally to Taiyuan in December, where it was engaged mainly in air defence duties.

Prior to the deployment of the Ki-27 in China, Soviet SBs, which had been provided to China from September 1937 and flown by Chinese aircrews or Russian volunteers, had enjoyed an advantage over the Japanese fighters in-theatre – the JAAF biplane Ki-10 and IJNAF monoplane Mitsubishi A5M. F P Polynin, one of the Soviet air group commanders, described how 'our SBs, exceeding in speed the Japanese fighters, were not threatened by encounters with them. Powerful armament gave us a very good chance of repulsing an attack, and if necessary, on account of our speed, we could break off contact with the opponent. We suffered greater losses from the poorly equipped and small Chinese aerodromes'.

The arrival of the Ki-27, with its superior speed and impressive rate-of-climb, forced the SB bombers to operate at higher altitudes of 25,000-29,000 ft, rather than their usual heights of 7000-13,000 ft. At higher altitudes the crews suffered problems with their poor oxygen equipment. Indeed, at least one SB was lost in China after the crew passed out from oxygen starvation.

The arrival of the Ki-27 in China did not escape the attention of the American Claire Lee Chennault, then serving as Chiang Kai-shek's chief air advisor. He first acquired solid intelligence about the new fighter, known to him as the Type 97, in 1939 after the Chinese captured an intact example and transported it to Chengtu. Here, Chennault was able to fly it in a series of tests against the Curtiss Hawk 75 (the export version of the US Army Air Corps' P-36 frontline fighter), the Gloster Gladiator and the Soviet I-16. He noted that it was 'one of the best aerobatic aeroplanes ever built', commenting that it 'climbs like a skyrocket and manoeuvres like a squirrel'. Chennault was later to remark that many of his AVG pilots were to find it 'more troublesome than the Zero (sic) because of its astonishing rate-of-climb and incredibly short turning radius'. He compiled a complete intelligence dossier on the type, which he sent to the US War Department before the outbreak of hostilities.

A Ki-27 Otsu with a distinctive black tail identifying the 10th Dokuritsu Hiko Chutai (Independent Air Squadron) is prepared for operations on an airfield in China. This photograph shows how the Toyota KC starter truck was used to start the aircraft's engine, with the drive shaft connected to a lug on the fighter's propeller hub. The lower wheel fairings of the Ki-27 have been removed to prevent mud clogging the axles and tipping the aircraft onto its nose (*Yasuho Izawa*)

COMBAT OVER NANCHENG

After the fall of Canton and Hankow in October 1938, the Chinese armies had retreated to Hengyang, Liuchow and Nancheng. The Chinese Air Force, severely depleted, withdrew to Szechuan and Kwangsi provinces, largely beyond the reach of the Japanese. These movements saw the beginning of a Japanese strategic bombing campaign (the brunt of which was borne by IJNAF units) against the Chinese cities of the interior, which reduced the opportunities for the Ki-27 to engage in fighter-versus-fighter combat because of the aircraft's modest range. JAAF bombers were escorted for a short while after they had taken off from Hankow, and upon their return.

From 26 December three JAAF heavy bomber units – the 12th and 98th Sentais, equipped with imported Fiat BR.20s, and the 60th Sentai, flying the Mitsubishi Ki-21 'Sally' – began targeting the Chinese city of Chungking, where the Nationalist government had established itself in exile.

To the Japanese, the Chinese Air Force, reduced to 135 fighters to defend four major cities, 'appeared to lack both fighting spirit and operational skill'. This was just as well, for the bombers were left unescorted over their targets because of the Ki-27's range limitations. Chungking was 485 miles from Hankow, and the Nakajima fighter's combat radius was only 280 miles. When IJNAF bombers took over the raids on Chungking, the JAAF bomber Sentai moved north to Yuncheng, in Shansi province. They flew their first mission from here on 12 February 1939 when Lanchow (now Lanzhou), some 422 miles away, was targeted.

Lanchow was the terminus of the Soviet-Chinese highway, thus making it a major centre for the receipt of Soviet war aid to Xi'an. This in turn meant that the city was defended in part by Soviet volunteer pilots. Here, the unescorted JAAF bombers encountered a more determined resistance in the air, losing aircraft to Chinese fighter opposition on 20 and 23 February.

Yuncheng had in turn come under attack from Chinese Vultee V-11/12 light bombers and SBs from 5 February, when ten Japanese aircraft were claimed destroyed on the ground. By 11 April the Chinese were claiming that the Japanese had withdrawn their bomber units from Yuncheng because of the losses inflicted by their air force.

The 64th Sentai HQ, along with the 1st and 2nd Chutai, had moved to Canton in November 1938, but its pilots had found little opportunity for aerial combat whilst flying mainly ground attack sorties and uneventful patrols. The 3rd Chutai, still detached from the 64th, moved to Taiyuan in March 1939 and to Yuncheng in April in response to the Chinese raids. On 29 April Lt Yoshio Sotomura led seven Ki-27s to Nancheng to sweep for Chinese aircraft that had been reported there. At this time the Chinese Air Force was staging forward from airfields beyond the reach of the JAAF whilst conducting ground attack sorties against Japanese army positions. No Chinese aircraft were found on the ground at Nancheng, but shortly thereafter, as the Japanese formation cruised at about

10,000 ft, a group of I-15s was seen climbing at 8000 ft over a nearby mountain ridge. Although reported as 20+ in number, they were actually six I-15bis of the 29th PS that had been scrambled from Nancheng prior to the arrival of the Japanese fighters.

The Chinese fighters, led by Capt Ma Kwok-lim, were flying in pairs, and the two flights of Japanese fighters immediately attacked the second and third pairs, while Capt Sotomura single-handedly attacked Capt Ma and his wingman, Lt Teng Chung-kwai. The I-15bis pilots attempted to provide mutual support for each other, but their opponents began a succession of gunnery runs on them using dive-and-zoom manoeuvres. These tactics exploited the climbing and turning capability of the Ki-27, being similar to the IJNAF's 'Hineri-komi' ('turning in') manoeuvre and the original 'Immelmann turn', where after firing the attacking aircraft would pull up steeply into a half loop and side-slip at the top, twisting into a dive to regain an attacking position behind and above the target aircraft.

One I-15bis from the third Chinese pair was almost immediately shot down, Lt Liu Sheng-fang being killed and his wingman, Lt Kung Shu-ming, taking hits in the upper wing of his fighter. Despite the damage Lt Kung was able to continuously evade the Ki-27s until they broke off the combat short of fuel. Three JAAF fighters had attacked the second

Sgt Shigeru Takuwa, second pilot of the 2nd Shotai of the 1st Chutai, 64th Sentai, flies a Ki-27 Otsu close to the camera aeroplane somewhere over China in early 1940. At this time the 1st Chutai was commonly known as the Maruta Detachment from the name of the Chutai leader, Capt Fumio Maruta, who had replaced Capt Sawada in March 1939. Note that the sliding canopy has been removed from the aircraft in an effort to improve visibility for the pilot. This was commonly done with the Ki-27 in China (*Yasuho Izawa*)

Pilots of the 2nd Chutai of the 64th Sentai in China in 1938. WO Tokuya Sudo, seated at the extreme right, was a graduate of the Juvenile Flying Soldier programme and had already claimed four victories as the wingman of Lt Iori Sakai (seated, second left) by the time this photograph was taken. WO Sudo would go on to become a stalwart of the unit over Nomonhan, being noted for his tenacity in flying multiple sorties in a single day and claiming a further six victories prior to being shot down and killed on 1 September 1939 (*Yasuho Izawa*)

An improvised wheel change in the field. The simple fixed undercarriage of the Ki-27, being easy to service and maintain, was an advantage on the primitive grass airfields in China that were frequently soaked by heavy downpours during the 'plum rains' of the east Asian monsoon. The distinctive graduated markings each side of the engine cowling were to facilitate machine gun synchronisation (*Summer*)

Chinese pair, killing Lt Chai Shi-wei. However, his wingman, Lt Liu Meng-chin, was able to fire a brief but accurate burst at one of the attacking fighters, which then crashed, killing Sgt Maj Takeji Harada. The remaining two Ki-27s then concentrated their attack on Lt Liu, who was forced to bail out of his badly damaged aircraft.

Meanwhile, Capt Sotomura had become engaged in a solitary slow-turning dogfight with Capt Ma and Lt Teng. During this engagement Ma was able to climb above the turning pair and conduct a fatal overhead pass on Sotomura, setting his wing tanks on fire. Sotomura tried to escape his pursuer but his burning aircraft was too badly damaged, allowing Ma to close to within 50 yards of the Ki-27 and open fire until his guns jammed. The JAAF fighter briefly flew on in level flight, before suddenly falling away and crashing, killing Capt Sotomura. After this fight Sgts Maj Takeshi Sasaki and Yoshio Matsuoka were each credited with two Chinese fighters shot down, whilst WO Hirokichi Matsushita and Sgt Maj Sadao Honda claimed one each. A total of 11 Chinese fighters were claimed shot down, against actual losses of only three and one damaged.

Within weeks of this action taking place the JAAF was to be distracted from the air war over China by Japan's emerging conflict with the USSR at Nomonhan, on the Mongolian-Manchurian border.

Sgt Maj Rinpei Tanaka of the 1st Chutai, 64th Sentai, stands by his Ki-27 Ko. This photograph provides a clear view of the stylised eagle motif applied beneath the cockpit of unit aircraft at this time. Sgt Maj Tanaka was a long serving veteran of the 2nd Daitai and 64th Sentai who was credited with at least five victories (*Rinpei Tanaka via Yasuho Izawa*)

THE CRUCIBLE OF NOMONHAN

Essentially, the Nomonhan conflict arose from a border dispute between Mongolia and Manchuria that was escalated by the mutual suspicion and animosity of the Soviet Union and Japan. Both sides concentrated and reinforced air resources in the disputed region, which led to increased encounters and a brief but intense period of air warfare during the summer of 1939. For the JAAF it was a proving ground for the Ki-27 fighter and led to the creation of aces who would go on to form an experienced cadre during the Pacific War, in terms of both air fighting and tactical doctrine, although some of the highest scoring aces were killed in the conflict.

In many respects the air war against the USSR provided both the sunrise and the sunset for the Ki-27, as it encountered the I-16 for the first time on a large scale. The Polikarpov machine was representative of a new generation of fighters, being fast-diving, armour-protected, heavily armed and with a retractable undercarriage. At first the Ki-27 was to prevail, its pilots being able to exploit the nimble machine's best characteristics – sparkling manoeuvrability and rate-of-climb – against poorly trained and led Soviet pilots, but in the long term the Nakajima fighter faced an increasingly arduous challenge. After their initial reverses the Soviets sent in a cadre of more experienced pilots, many of them veterans of the Spanish Civil War, whilst the capability of the I-16 was improved (see *Aircraft of the Aces 95* for further details). For the JAAF many lessons were learned, these being incorporated both into the design and development of new aircraft types and in evolution of tactical doctrine.

Although the complex ground war of the Nomonhan conflict is beyond the scope of this study, it should be noted that the fighting between the Red Army and Japanese troops was more often the imperative that governed the aerial activity of both sides, as each tried to wrest tactical control of the skies over the battlefield and secure strategic air supremacy by striking at the opponent's airfields.

Ki-27s of the 24th Sentai, the first JAAF fighter unit to go into action over Nomonhan, are prepared for operations in typical Manchurian surroundings of flat grass plains and big sky (*Picarella Collection*)

Ki-27s of the 24th Sentai await action in a typical Nomonhan setting. These aircraft appear to be a mixture of Ko and Otsu types (*James F Lansdale*)

The first Ki-27 unit to see action against the Soviets over Nomonhan was the 24th Sentai, which provided the fighter element of an ad hoc tactical unit designated a Rinji-Hikotai (Provisional Air Group) that was formed from Lt Gen Tetsuji Giga's 2nd Hikoshidan and placed under the command of the 24th Sentai's CO, Lt Col Kojiro Matsumura. In addition to the 19-20 Ki-27s of the 24th Sentai, Matsumura also commanded six Mitsubishi Ki-30 light bombers and six Mitsubishi Ki-15-I reconnaissance aircraft from the 10th Sentai.

The 24th had been stationed at Hailar, in Manchuria, since September 1938, having been established there with two Chutai following formation at Harbin earlier that same month from a nucleus provided by the 11th Sentai. The 24th moved to Kanjur Miao airfield on 17 May and began operations three days later.

Although the JAAF was initially restricted to performing patrols within the border area, with pilots having been instructed to react only to incursions by Mongolian or Soviet aircraft, action occurred on the very first day the 24th started operational flying. A flight of 1st Chutai Ki-27s under the command of the Sentai leader, Lt Col Matsumra, reportedly encountered a Polikarpov R-5 reconnaissance biplane escorted by two I-16s over the Khalkhin Gol River. The two I-16s immediately fled, whereupon Lt Soichi Suzuki and MSgt Hideo Tatsumi shot the R-5 down after six gunnery runs. This victory is not supported in Soviet records, and it might have become confused with a similar claim made the following day – or perhaps the R-5 was a Mongolian aircraft.

On 21 May Sgt Chiyoji Saito of the 2nd Chutai also claimed an R-5 that was flying in support of the 6th Mongolian Cavalry Division over the disputed border area. Its pilot, Supron, was killed in the attack, but the observer, Arkhipov, managed to bail out. The loss of the aeroplane was recorded as the second JAAF victory of the conflict, and the first for Chiyoji Saito (not to be confused with fellow ace Shogo Saito of the 1st Chutai, 24th Sentai), who would eventually claim 21 victories over Nomonhan and ultimately as many as 28 following additional action in the Philippines, China and New Guinea, where he acquired a reputation as a P-38 killer. On 10 June 1943 he collided with his Chutai leader, Lt Tadashi Koga, while landing at But airfield when vision was obscured by clouds of dust. Saito was badly injured but Koga was killed, the former blaming himself for the accident and telling other pilots that he would never return to Japan alive. Indeed, he did not. Saito was killed over Wewak on 20 August 1943 attempting to intercept B-24 Liberator bombers and their P-38 Lightning escorts.

On 22 May 1939, just after noon, another 24th Sentai flight led by Capt Saiji Kani (the 1st Chutai leader), with wingman Sgt Maj Tatsumi and third pilot Sgt Maj Yutaka Kimura, claimed to have encountered three

Pilots of the 24th Sentai relax around a Toyota KC starter truck in between sorties over Nomonhan. This photograph is well known, but the pilots are seldom identified. Sitting in the cab is Chiyoji Saito, who claimed 21 victories over Nomonhan and at least seven more during the Pacific War, before being killed in action on 20 August 1943 over Wewak, New Guinea. Standing to the left is Kira Katsuaki, who was credited with nine victories over Nomonhan and 21 in total. On the right, reading a book, is Goro Nishihara, and next to him, seated, is Koji Ishizawa, a 12-victory ace over Nomonhan who, like Katsuaki, would continue to claim kills in the Ki-27 over the Philippines and in China during 1942. Ishizawa then flew over New Guinea with the 24th, surviving to war's end with the 105th Sentai. His final victory tally is unknown (*Yasuho Izawa*)

I-16s that had crossed the border. Having quickly shot all three Soviet fighters down, the Japanese formation was then attacked by 'six more' Polikarpovs, one of which was shot down by Sgt Maj Tatsumi. In fact, the JAAF fighters had been bounced by three I-16s and two I-15s of 70th IAP (*Istrebitelniy Aviatsionnyi Polk* – Fighter Aviation Regiment), whose pilots claimed to have encountered five 'I-96s' – the Mitsubishi A5M, which was the IJNAF's principal fighter at the time, being similar in configuration to the Ki-27.

One of the Soviet pilots, Lysenko, flying an I-16, attacked Tatsumi, who flung his Ki-27 into a tight left-hand vertical turn. Lysenko tried to follow the Japanese pilot but Tatsumi was able to turn inside the I-16 and shoot it down, killing the Soviet pilot. Both Kani and Kimura also claimed their first victories during this engagement, and they would ultimately increase their tallies to nine apiece over Nomonhan. However, on this occasion, only Lysenko's I-16 was reported as having been lost, with the remaining Soviet fighters (including the trio of I-16s initially encountered) returning to their airfield despite damage.

Capt Kani was a 27-year-old ex-cadet officer and native of Ishikawa who would not survive Nomonhan whilst Yutaka Kimura was 20 years old and would survive the war to fly helicopters in the JSDAF, retiring in 1960.

On 24 May 1939, in response to what was seen as escalating Soviet air incursions, Col Yudjiro Noguchi's 11th Sentai moved 20 Ki-27s of the 1st and 3rd Chutai to Caiyansuo from Harbin to participate in JAAF operations over Nomonhan. This was part of a general reinforcement that saw the 12th Hikodan HQ under Maj Gen Eiji Higashi take control of the two fighter units, the main body of an airfield battalion transferred in to provide enhanced ground support facilities and elements of a radio intelligence unit established.

The 11th had been re-designated as a Sentai from the 11th Rentai in August 1938, and it was

NCO pilots of the 24th Sentai during the Nomonhan fighting. At left is Sgt Yutaka Kimura, who flew in the lead element of Capt Saiji Kana's 1st Chutai. On 22 May 1939 he scored his first victory (an I-16), and on 22 June he was to claim six more Soviet fighters in a fight against the odds, although his Ki-27 was left badly damaged. After this epic fight Kimura was appointed wingman to the Sentai commander, Lt Col Kojiro Matsumura, but on 24 June he was badly wounded whilst attacking SB bombers – he had shot one of them down just moments earlier. Kimura's final score was nine victories, and he survived the war to serve in the JSDAF (*Yasuho Izawa*)

Shoji Kurono was another Nomonhan 12-victory ace in the 24th Sentai, being noted for his expert marksmanship. Here, he is seen wearing typical winter flying gear for a Ki-27 pilot. Aged 33, Kurono was one of the older pilots in the unit. Indeed, he had been seriously wounded during the Manchurian conflict of 1932. Kurono joined the 2nd Chutai from the reserve, and after Nomonhan he served in the 3rd Chutai training new pilots. From 1940 he was a flying instructor at Akeno and Hitachi, although he was to experience further combat with the 112th Sentai flying the Ki-100 during the last months of the war. During these air defence sorties the doughty 39-year-old veteran claimed a B-29 and F6F shot down and another F6F damaged (*Yasuho Izawa*)

Sgt Maj Shogo Saito (not to be confused with Chiyoji Saito) was the most successful pilot of the 24th Sentai during the Nomonhan fighting, claiming 25 victories. Having been credited with two I-15s destroyed during his first combat on 26 May 1939, he made 'ace in a day' on 22 June by claiming five I-16s, including one which he reported deliberately ramming. After Nomonhan, Saito flew as a warrant officer with the 24th Sentai over the Philippines, and then went on to see action in the Ki-61 with the 78th Sentai over New Guinea, claiming a B-24. He was killed in ground combat on 2 July 1944 as his unit, now without aircraft, retreated on foot (*Yasuho Izawa*)

unusual in having a complement of four rather than three Chutai. It was destined to become the highest-scoring JAAF Ki-27 fighter unit of the Nomonhan conflict, with its 1st Chutai claiming 180 of the 530 victories recorded by the unit – more than half of the JAAF's total claims. At Nomonhan the 11th Sentai would generate no fewer than 21 aces with more than ten victory claims, only a few of whom would gain recognition in the West.

During its first patrol along the disputed border (on 24 May) the 11th's 3rd Chutai encountered four I-15s over the hills of Hamar-Daba. Twenty-four-year-old Sgt Saburo Kimura, from a mountain village in Yamagata Prefecture (and who is not to be confused with fellow ace Yutaka Kimura of the 24th Sentai), attacked one of them, closing to within 30 ft and shooting the Polikarpov down for his first victory.

On 26 May a formation from the 24th Sentai's 1st Chutai encountered Soviet aircraft over Lake Buyr-nuir. During a scattered fight 21-year-old Sgt Maj Shogo Saito became separated from his formation, and when he attempted to join up with what he thought was a friendly Shotai (flight) from his own unit, he discovered that they were in fact Soviet I-15bis. Quickly climbing above them, Saito then dived at the formation and claimed to have shot down two biplane fighters for his first recorded victories, before disengaging and returning home. Soviet records do not appear to admit these losses.

Shogo Saito would duly become the 24th Sentai's leading ace over Nomonhan, claiming 25 victories. He continued to fly with the Sentai during the initial attack on the Philippines, but in March 1942 was transferred to the 78th Sentai and later commissioned, subsequently flying the Ki-61 over New Guinea, where he claimed a B-24. Saito was to die in ground combat on 2 July 1944 after the 78th had been denuded of all of its aircraft.

On 27 May 1939 the 11th Sentai was in action once again when a flight of three Ki-27s cruised provocatively over a Mongolian landing ground at Hamar-Daba that had recently seen the arrival of eight I-16s of 1st IAE (*Istrebitelnaya Aviaeskadrilya* – Fighter Squadron) of 22nd IAP from Tamsag Bulag in response to recent Japanese air incursions. The Soviets scrambled six I-16s in pursuit of the Ki-27s, but the fighter pilots took off without their leader Kutsevalov who, together with one of his pilots, was unable to start his engine. The I-16s, climbing individually rather than in formation through 6500 ft, ran straight into two more flights of 11th Sentai Ki-27s approaching at almost 10,000 ft. The Japanese pilots dived at the Soviet machines, attacking in a tight, disciplined formation that sliced through the climbing I-16s just as the three Ki-27s that had

Pilots of the 11th Sentai's 2nd Chutai pose for a group photograph at Harbin, Manchuria, in early 1939. The 2nd Chutai claimed 124 victories over Nomonhan. Its leader, Capt Toshio Sakagawa, is seated, third from left. Although he missed most of the Nomonhan fighting, he would command the Kawasemi Butai (the 47th IFC) for battle testing of the pre-production Ki-44 at the start of the Pacific War, and later gain fame as the commander of the 25th Sentai in China, claiming a total of more than 15 victories. Seated at left with sunglasses is Mamoru Hanada (17 victories), and immediately to the right of Sakagawa, also seated, is Yamato Takiyama (six victories), who later commanded the 104th Sentai. In the back row, standing at far left, is Akira Ina (nine victories), then Taro Kobayashi (ten victories). Standing, third from right, is Hitoshi Tobita (seven victories over Nomonhan and an RAF Vildebeest claimed over Endau, Malaya). Standing, second from right, is Tokuyasu Ishizuka (12 victories over Nomonhan) and next to him is Cpl Haruo Takagaki, the youngest of the 11th Sentai aces with 15 victories over Nomonhan and two over New Guinea (*Akira Ina via Yasuho Izawa*)

lured the Soviets up returned to join the fray. The lead Polikarpov pilot, Cherenkov, tried to form a defensive circle against the Ki-27s but most of his men dived away in confusion.

The JAAF fighters were under the command of the 1st Chutai leader Capt Kenji Shimada, who would claim three of the I-16s shot down as the first of his 27 Nomonhan victories. Shimada was 29 years old, born in Tokyo and a graduate of the Army Air Academy.

Another pilot in the 1st Chutai formation, 25-year-old WO Hiromichi Shinohara (the son of a farmer from Suzumenomiya, in Tochigi Prefecture, and an ex-cavalryman who had fought in the Manchurian Incident of 1932), claimed four I-16s downed, including the aircraft of Cherenkov, who was killed in the encounter. Shinohara would go on to become the highest scoring Japanese ace of the conflict with 58 victories, but would not survive it. He kept a diary, and was adamant that his claims were scrupulously recorded. 'There are no probables in my score', Shinohara wrote. 'My definition of a victory is that the aircraft fell in flames. No others were counted'.

One of the Soviet pilots, Savchenko, was reported to have damaged a Ki-27, which fled the scene trailing smoke. He was then killed, however, trying to crash-land his I-16, the fighter's engine being either faulty or damaged. Another pilot, Pyankov, was wounded in the engagement, but managed to force land his burning I-16 and escape the subsequent strafing attack (some accounts refer to him bailing out). His adversary might have been Sgt Maj Eisaku Suzuki, who reported pursuing an I-16 over the Khalkha River and forcing it to land, whereupon he strafed the fighter until it burned. This was Suzuki's first victory of 11 claimed.

Two other Soviet pilots dived away early on in the action and force landed on the steppe below, whilst a third managed to return with his I-16 badly shot up. The Japanese claimed nine Polikarpovs shot down (despite only six having been encountered) for no losses, with more than one of the victorious pilots probably claiming the same enemy aircraft. The two I-16s that dived away to force land may have also been seen as victories by the attacking JAAF pilots.

During the early morning light of the following day, a flight of three I-15bis from 70th IAP were caught by the 11th Sentai's 1st Chutai and shot down, with pilots Voznesenkiy, Ivanchenko and Chekmarev being

One of the legendary aces of the 11th, and better known in the West, was Capt Kenji Shimada, leader of the 1st Chutai. He is seen here (left) with his eight victory star marked Ki-27 Otsu. Of the 180 enemy aircraft claimed over Nomonhan by the 11th's 1st Chutai, 27 were credited to Shimada. He and his wingman, Sgt Maj Bunji Yoshiyama, failed to return from a sortie on 15 September 1939 – the last day of the fighting in Nomonhan. This aircraft appears to be fitted with a gun camera atop the port wing (*Yasuho Izawa*)

killed. These machines had been part of a larger force brought to readiness at Tamsag Bulag and scrambled at 0700 hrs in response to Japanese air attacks against ground forces, only to then be recalled. The three downed I-15bis were the last Soviet aircraft still aloft when they were bounced.

Capt Shimada claimed one of the I-15bis and WO Shinohara another (the first of five Polikarpovs he was to claim that day), together with an R-5 reconnaissance biplane. The pilot of the I-15bis that he shot down managed to bail out, but Shinohara deliberately cut the cords of his parachute with the wingtip of his Ki-27. The other pilot to make a claim was Sgt Maj Bunji Yoshiyama, who was credited with his first victory. Yoshiyama, who often flew as wingman to Capt Shimada, would eventually tally 20 victories, thus becoming the third ranking ace of the 1st Chutai during Nomonhan. He too would be another top pilot destined not to survive the conflict.

At about 1000 hrs that same day (28 May) 22nd IAP sent ten I-15bis aloft, led by Capt Balashov, to patrol the Khalkhin-Gol River in response to Japanese incursions. This was the regiment's second sortie of the day, having been scrambled earlier alongside 70th IAP. The I-15bis formation was attacked by both Chutai of the 11th Sentai, under the command of Col Noguchi. From their superior height, the 18 Ki-27s slammed head-on into the Soviet formation, which scattered, with most of the pilots attempting to dive away. Balashov was wounded in the head in the initial pass, but he managed to return to Tamsag Bulag, as did Gavrilov in a badly shot up aircraft. Four Soviet pilots were killed, however, including the deputy leader Myagkov, who dived to ground level in his burning aircraft and managed to extinguish the flames, only to then be shot down by a pursuing Ki-27. Two pilots were wounded in the action, force-landing their aircraft, another managed to bail out and return to the regiment four days later and the final pilot was posted as missing.

11th Sentai Ki-27s on a Nomonhan landing ground. The 11th was to claim 530 victories during the Nomonhan fighting, which was just about half of the total victories credited to the JAAF during the conflict. The actual number of Soviet aircraft lost is a matter of controversy, but recent studies suggest 207 machines were destroyed in aerial combat, of which 160 were Polikarpov fighters. JAAF Ki-27 losses in the air totalled 62 (*Author collection*)

From the 1st Chutai, Shinohara claimed three I-15bis and Yoshiyama one, whilst the 3rd Chutai's Sgt Maj Tomio Hanada downed two and Sgt Majs Saburo Kimura and 22-year-old Masao Ashida one each for their second and first victories of 19 and 11, respectively. The 23-year-old Hanada, a native of Akune, in Kagoshima Prefecture, would become the leading Nomonhan ace of the 11th Sentai's 3rd Chutai with 25 victory claims. A serious and taciturn character, he spent hours studying the techniques of aerial combat and used model aircraft to demonstrate them to fellow pilots.

A Ki-27 Otsu is attended by groundcrew in the field, the fighter perhaps being prepared for starting. Note that this aircraft is carrying extra fuel tanks beneath the wings and the lower undercarriage fairings have been removed. The harsh operating conditions for which the simplicity of the Ki-27 was well suited are evident (*Summer*)

From the Japanese formation only Lt Mitsusoshi was shot down, but he managed to bail out. Having seen his comrade-in-arms land in Mongolian territory, 2Lt Tomoari Hasegawa made the first 'rescue landing' in the Ki-27 so as to extricate him from enemy territory. The Nakajima fighter had a hatch in the belly through which the fuselage interior behind the pilot's seat could be accessed. In this cramped location, several downed JAAF pilots would be plucked from the Nomonhan battlefields and flown to safety. This incident, and others like it, would inspire a similar rescue scene in the 1940 Toho war film *Moyuro Ozora* ('The Flaming Sky').

Following these Soviet reversals in combat, there was a temporary ban introduced on further sorties by the Polikarpov-equipped regiments, resulting in a lull in the air fighting. The Soviet command then brought in a cadre of 48 experienced fighter pilots, many of whom were veterans of the Spanish Civil War that would subsequently become aces over Nomonhan. Aircraft losses were also replenished so that by the middle of June 70th IAP had 60 I-16s and 24 I-15bis on strength, whilst 22nd IAP had 35 I-16s and 32 I-15bis.

The JAAF also used this pause in the fighting to transfer the 1st Sentai to Manchuria from Japan in early June. This unit, consisting of only two Chutai and 23 Ki-27s, was under the command of Lt Col Toshio Kato (not to be confused with future ace Tateo Kato). Having only just been re-equipped with the new fighter, the 1st would fight as part of the 7th Hikodan under Maj Gen Hisao Hozoji. The latter also boasted 12 imported BR.20 bombers (known as the 'I-Shiki') of the 12th Sentai and the 15th Sentai's mixed complement of six Mitsubishi Ki-15 reconnaissance aircraft and eight Tachikawa Ki-36 direct cooperation machines. In addition, the 9th Hikodan, under Maj Gen Ikkaku Shimono, had 12 Ki-21 bombers of the 61st Sentai and another mixed complement unit (the 10th Sentai) equipped with six Ki-15s and six Ki-30 light bombers.

Over Nomonhan, the 1st Sentai would generate no fewer than 12 Ki-27 aces, the top Gekitsui-oh in the unit being 24-year-old Sgt Maj Mitsuyoshi Tarui with 28 victories. Although little known in the West, Sgt Maj Tarui would become the second ranking Japanese ace over Nomonhan and subsequently claim at least ten more victories over New Guinea whilst flying the Kawasaki Ki-61 with the 68th Sentai.

The lull continued until 17 June 1939 when air activity began to build up again as Soviet reconnaissance flights probed the border areas. It rapidly intensified when Japanese troops unsuccessfully attacked Red Army positions at Depden Sume on 20 June. This was followed by a series of attacks on Japanese positions by Soviet aircraft. On 22 June the air fighting re-erupted in earnest with the biggest encounter of the conflict to date.

The day of action began with a fighter sweep by 18 Ki-27s of the 24th Sentai over the disputed border area. A Soviet fighter force of 12 I-16s and nine I-15bis of 22nd IAP scrambled in response, pilots in the latter machines climbing warily to 13,000 ft in formation behind their leader, Capt Stepanov. The I-16s, led by Lt Savkin, became dangerously strung out, however, and upon meeting the Japanese fighters they found themselves at a height disadvantage. The JAAF pilots had managed to climb above their opponents, before diving through the Soviet formation in a punishing attack that left Savkin wounded and with little choice but to force land.

The I-15bis formation then joined the fight, which developed into a swirling aerial battle. Three biplane fighters were forced down, including the aircraft flown by Stepanov. Moments later a substantial force of 70th IAP I-16s arrived, causing the Japanese pilots, who were now low on both ammunition and fuel, to break off the engagement. A series of low-level running fights followed in which the Ki-27s attempted to evade and outfly their faster pursuers. A JAAF fighter pilot recalled that this was no easy feat when pursued by an I-16;

'The 97-Sen was easy to fly and very agile. If a pursuer was seen it was easy to climb quickly and turn to follow him, but it could not be dived too steeply or too fast without excessive vibration and it became difficult to take aim properly. Diving away from a fight was always dangerous because the "gadfly" [I-16] could dive more strongly, and vigilance was necessary.'

Capt A S Nikolayev, who flew an I-153 during the latter stages of the conflict, gained a similar impression of the Ki-27 in combat;

'[The] I-97 [Ki-27] dived steeply for less than 700-1000 m, then the enemy pilot would stop the pursuit. During interrogation captured [Japanese] airmen were asked why they were diving steeply, but not for very long. They said that there was considerable vibration, especially [from] their wings, and the engine rapidly cooled off and could even stop. There was an incident during combat when the wing of [an] I-97 was torn off during diving. The wing disintegrated after a dive of 500-700m. The possibility of wing damage during pursuit was impossible as fire was aimed at the cockpit. Eyewitnesses confirmed that it was a brand new aircraft.'

Officers of the 24th Sentai photographed during the Nomonhan fighting on 24 June 1939. They are, from left to right, Sentai commander Lt Col Kojiro Matsumura, 1st Chutai leader Capt Saiji Kani (a nine-victory ace who was killed in action on 29 July 1939) and Lt Hyoe Yonaga (a 16-victory Nomonhan ace who also flew with the Sentai over the Philippines and south China during 1942) (*Yasuho Izawa*)

1Lt Furokawa, leading the 2nd Shotai in the 24th's 2nd Chutai, was wounded during the fight on 22 June. His wingman, 20-year-old MSgt Katsuaki Kira, downed the I-16 that had attacked Furokawa, but used up all his ammunition in doing so. He then managed to deter another I-16 and an I-15bis with some innovative aerobatics after they too attempted to attack Furokawa. Kira then joined two more Ki-27 pilots that had also exhausted their ammunition in an unarmed attack on two I-15bis, which crashed as they attempted to evade the wildly aggressive manoeuvres of the Japanese pilots. The trio of JAAF pilots then buzzed Mongolian troops that were digging in on the ground, before heading home. The third pilot in Furokawa's Shotai, Sgt Maj Koji Ishizawa, claimed two and returned from the fight unscathed, going on to claim 11 victories over Nomonhan.

The 2nd Chutai leader Capt Shigenobu Morimoto was not so lucky, being killed in the engagement when he was shot down by an I-15bis. Sgt Chiyoji Saito, flying as the third pilot in Morimoto's flight, claimed three aircraft destroyed and one probable. 1Lt Hyoe Yonaga, leading the third Shotai, was credited with one Soviet fighter shot down and one probable, whilst Sgt Maj Goro Nishihara, who was flying as the third pilot in Yonaga's flight, also claimed three destroyed and one probable.

Ki-27s from the 24th's 1st Chutai had pursued the Soviet aircraft fleeing from the first encounter across the Khalkha River, where they were engaged by 70th IAP I-16s joining the fight. The 1st Chutai leader, Capt Saiji Kani, and his wingman, Sgt Maj Tatsumi, each claimed an I-16 destroyed. Capt Kani recorded his impressions of the action as follows;

'How many enemy aircraft there were, but we had courage, like eagles pursuing swallows, and overwhelmed the enemy. At about 5.30 pm I spotted 25-26 more flying at about 2000 m. On the first pass one was going down in flames, and one by one others went down the same way. More new enemy aircraft appeared and entered the battle – they were all around – we left the area and returned [home]. There were many hits in the wings and tail of my aircraft.'

Sgt Maj Yutaka Kimura, flying as the third pilot in Capt Kani's flight, also claimed a Soviet fighter in the initial attack, but then climbed away when the Japanese formations were scattered by the arrival of the I-16s. Re-joining the melee, he aggressively attacked every I-16 that he could see, claiming another five destroyed until he was overcome by fumes from his damaged and leaking fuel tanks, his aircraft having been hit 21 times. Kimura recovered at low level and headed home, being pursued by eight I-16s. Convinced that offence was the best form of defence, he repeatedly turned into his opponents during a 30-minute running battle, claiming to have shot down yet another I-16 before finally escaping his enemies. Following this epic combat Kimura was appointed wingman to the Sentai commander, Lt Col Matsumura.

Sgt Maj Shogo Saito claimed four I-16s after 70th IAP engaged the Ki-27s, including one where the pilot landed immediately upon being attacked. Saito then used up his remaining ammunition strafing this aircraft – an act that nearly cost him his life when he found himself out of ammunition and boxed in by two flights of I-16s that were determined to force him down over Mongolian territory. Choosing his moment, Saito suddenly lifted the nose of his Ki-27 and turned sharply, flying straight towards an I-16. The startled Soviet pilot tried to dive beneath Saito as he climbed straight at him, but his fin collided with the Japanese pilot's starboard tailplane and the crippled I-16 fell away as the remaining Polikarpov fighters scattered in confusion. Saito managed to nurse his badly damaged Ki-27 home.

Sgt Maj Goro Nishihara relaxes on the grass beside a 24th Sentai Ki-27. The aircraft behind him has two stripes on the fin and four on the rudder, signifying '24', but it has not had individual katakana character 'su' applied (see Profile 1). Nishihara claimed a total of 12 victories over Nomonhan (*Yasuho Izawa*)

1Lt Shoichi Suzuki, who had claimed the first JAAF victory of the Nomonhan conflict on 20 May and then added a second victory to his tally on 26 May, claimed five Soviet fighters on 22 June prior to being wounded in the right wrist. Suzuki then attempted to withdraw from the fighting, only to be chased by three more communist fighters. Turning to engage them, Suzuki claimed them all shot down for a total of eight victories in one day! He was subsequently hospitalised for nearly a month, eventually returning to combat duties on 21 July.

In total, the 24th Sentai's Ki-27 pilots claimed 49 victories on 22 June, whilst the Soviets admitted the loss of only 13 aircraft (ten I-15bis and three I-16s) and the death of 11 pilots, including 22nd IAP commander Maj Nikolai Glazykin, whilst claiming 39 Japanese aircraft downed. The Japanese admitted seven Ki-27s had been lost with four pilots killed, including Sgt Maj Yotutaka (Shiko) Miyajima who had force landed during the fight. Miyajima wandered through the steppe for four days without food or water before being captured by a Mongolian cavalry patrol. Held as a prisoner by the Soviets for ten months, Miyajima was court-martialed upon being repatriated to Japan for desertion under enemy fire and sentenced to two years and ten months imprisonment. He was not released until 31 December 1942.

Following the 22 June combat and the wounding of 1Lt Furokawa, 1Lt Yonaga took command of the 2nd Chutai until new leader Capt Shoichi Tashiro was appointed at the end of the month, whereupon he reverted to leading a Shotai. Yonaga survived Nomonhan with a total of 16 victory claims, after which he spent a year as a flying instructor at Akeno before being posted back to the 24th Sentai in July 1941, taking command of the 2nd Chutai in the fighting over the Philippines. Although he continued to fly the Ki-27 in combat over south China during the summer of 1942, Yonaga made no further claims through to the end of World War 2.

In response to the resumption of air combat, and a perceived threat from increasing numbers of Soviet aircraft, the JAAF reinforced its air assets in forward areas by moving up additional units, including the remaining Chutai of the 11th and 1st Sentais, also equipped with the Ki-27.

The 4th Chutai of the 11th made its combat debut on 24 June when it went to the aid of the 24th Sentai, which had engaged Soviet fighters that had been escorting SB bombers. Two of the I-16 formations were led by Spanish Civil War veterans, and a third group of eight Polikarpovs soon joined the fight. The tables were quickly turned on the Ki-27 pilots thanks to the overwhelming number of I-16s. Yutaka Kimura, flying as wingman for the CO of the 24th Sentai, shot down one aircraft to raise his score to nine but was then wounded. Barely escaping from the fight, he was hospitalised and took no further part in the Nomonhan fighting.

The oldest and most stalwart flyer in the 4th Chutai was 29-year-old WO Riichi Ito who would claim 16 victories during the conflict – his first came during the hard-fought action of 24 June. After Nomonhan he served as a flying instructor but fell ill with tuberculosis and eventually died in 1950. Ito's Chutai leader, Capt Jozo Iwahashi, went one better than him on the 24th when he claimed the first two of his 20 successes during the Nomonhan conflict. Becoming one of the Chutai's leading aces, Iwahashi was subsequently awarded the 4th Grade Order of the Kinshi Kunsho (The Order of the Golden Kite) for his bravery and leadership in combat. After serving as a flying instructor at Akeno and a test pilot at Fussa, he became the chief test pilot for the Nakajima Ki-84 Hayate.

In March 1944 Iwahashi was made CO of the 22nd Sentai, the first unit to be equipped with the Hayate. Leading this unit to China in August 1944, he claimed a P-40 destroyed prior to his death during a strafing attack on Xian on 21 September. Iwahashi's final victory tally is uncertain, but is believed to exceed 21 claims.

Capt Iwahashi's wingman on 24 June 1939 was 27-year-old Sgt Maj Shoji Kato, who claimed no fewer than six of the 12 victories credited to Ki-27 pilots during this engagement. His tally would eventually reach 23 by the time the Nomonhan conflict had come to an end. In July 1941 Kato graduated as a second lieutenant from the Army Air Academy, only to be killed in a flying accident on 6 September 1941.

The third pilot in Capt Iwahashi's flight on 24 June was 21-year-old Cpl Naoharu Shiromoto, who claimed his first victory in the initial attack on the I-16s and was then pursued down to low-level by Soviet fighters. Barely escaping with his life, Shiromoto went on to claim a further ten victories over Nomonhan before his unit was transferred to the 1st Sentai to become its 3rd Chutai. Remaining with this unit, he saw further action during the Malayan campaign, over New Guinea and in the air defence of Japan (see Chapter 3 and *Aircraft of the Aces 100* for further details).

His classmate Cpl Jiro Okuda also claimed his first victory on the 24th. Both pilots had been trained by Capt Iwahashi, and although participating in operations with him, their rank meant that they were still considered to be under tuition in the finer points of combat flying. Okuda would become another stalwart pilot of the 4th Chutai, claiming a total of 14 victories by the time of his death on 12 August 1939 in a fight against overwhelming odds.

A third corporal flying with the 4th Chutai that day was Rikio Shibata, who would also claim 14 victories over Nomonhan but would survive the fighting there to further his career as one of the leading aces of the 85th Sentai, flying the Ki-44 (see *Aircraft of the Aces 100*). His score had reached 27 by the time of his death in action over Hankow on 18 December 1944.

On 25 June 1939 it was the 1st Sentai's turn to engage Soviet fighters when the 3rd Shotai (led by 1Lt Fujio Honma) of the 1st Chutai, en route to Caiyansuo airfield from Kanjur Miao, spotted a group of I-15s and began manoeuvring into a favourable position to attack them. Moments later they were attacked by a larger force of Soviet fighters. In the confused dogfight that followed Sgt Maj Mitsuyoshi Tarui and Cpl Arai each claimed to have shot down two Soviet fighters before successfully escaping. Tarui's air combat prowess flying the Ki-27 in the 1st Sentai would continue during the 1941-42 offensive against Malaya and the East Indies.

Two days later, on the 27th, the Japanese attempted a knockout blow by sending bombers, escorted by fighters, to target the Soviet airfields around Tamsag Bulag. The JAAF force, personally accompanied by Lt Gen Tetsuji Giga in an unarmed Ki-15 reconnaissance aircraft, consisted of 12 I-Shiki (BR.20) heavy bombers of the 12th Sentai, nine Ki-21 heavy bombers of the 61st Sentai and nine Ki-30 light bombers of the 10th and 16th Sentais, escorted by 74 Ki-27s of the 1st, 11th and 24th Sentais. The 24th provided

Cpl Jiro Okuda of the 4th Chutai, 11th Sentai stands proudly before a Ki-27 Otsu during the summer of 1939 – possibly the aircraft of the 4th Chutai leader Capt Jozo Iwahashi, who claimed 20 victories over Nomonhan. Okuda had claimed 14 kills over Nomonhan by the time he perished in combat on 12 August 1939. The 11th Sentai emblem was a lightning bolt painted on the fin and rudder in the Chutai colour, in this case green (*Yasuho Izawa*)

The second ranking ace of the 1st Sentai over Nomonhan was WO Hitoshi Asano of the 2nd Chutai, who claimed 22 victories. After Nomonhan he graduated from the Army Air Academy as a second lieutenant. Following a spell as an instructor, Asano served in the 248th Sentai over New Guinea until he was wounded during a bombing raid on 25 November 1943. Sent back to Japan to recuperate, he eventually served out the rest of the war as a flying instructor (*Yasuho Izawa*)

top cover at 18,000 ft for the bomber formations (although the Sentai's fighters were late taking off and had to race to catch up), the 1st flew close escort and the 11th trailed behind the main body of aircraft and conducted follow-up strafing attacks.

During the close escort flight to the targets Sgt Maj Tarui's two Shotai comrades collided and his leader, 1Lt Honma, was forced to bail out over Soviet territory. Tarui landed without hesitation and successfully rescued Honma. The remaining close escorts from the 1st Sentai were confronted by Soviet fighters that took off piecemeal to attempt interceptions.

Watching the air battle from above in frustration as the top cover fighters remained steadfastly with the bombers, 24th Sentai commander Lt Col Kojiro Matsumura described the success enjoyed by his counterparts in the 1st Sentai as being as 'easy as twisting an infant's hand'.

The leading scorer to emerge from this one-sided action was 28-year-old WO Hitoshi Asano, who was flying as the third pilot in the Shotai led by Lt Col Toshio Kato, CO of the 1st Sentai. Asano described how they surprised a gaggle of climbing I-15s strung out in irregular formation. Diving through the Soviet fighters with his guns blazing, he claimed no fewer than eight shot down for the first of the 22 victories that would make him the 1st Sentai's leading ace over Nomonhan.

Sgt Maj Isamu Hosono also flew regularly as Lt Col Kato's third pilot during this period (although not on 27 June), and he was to be credited with 21 victories over Nomonhan. Hosono went on to claim five more victories flying the fighter with the 25th Sentai over China before deliberately diving his fatally damaged fighter into a river on 6 October 1943.

Also experiencing his first dogfight on 27 June 1939 was 22-year-old Sgt Maj Misao Inoue of the 1st Sentai's 2nd Chutai. He would claim eight victories in the campaign before being badly wounded on 25 July. In the 1st Sentai's 1st Chutai, Sgt Maj Muneyoshi Motojima claimed the first of his 16 victories in the Nomonhan fighting on 27 June, as did Sgt Maj Takayori Kodama of the 2nd Chutai, who was credited with two kills. He would eventually claim 11 victories over Nomonhan.

Despite trailing the main formation, the 11th Sentai soon became embroiled in the swirling dogfights on 27 June. Leading the way in terms of aerial success on this date was the 1st Chutai's Sgt Maj Bunji Yoshiyama, who claimed three I-16s and an I-15 destroyed. During his return flight home he landed behind enemy lines and rescued Sgt Maj Eisaku Suzuki whose damaged Ki-27 had come down near Lake Buyr Nuir.

WO Koichi Iwase, who had missed the early fighting over Nomonhan after being injured in a landing accident, was flying as wingman to WO Shinohara. Despite using up all of his ammunition during the fighting, he failed to make a single claim and his Ki-27 was struck at least ten times by enemy gunfire.

In the 2nd Chutai, 2Lt Yamato Takiyama, who was also experiencing combat for the first time, claimed a single I-16 shot down whilst

Sgt Maj Isamu Hosono, seen here in winter flying gear standing in front of the Ki-27 assigned to the 1st Chutai leader, Capt Shigetoshi Inoue, at Saienjo airfield, was a 1st Sentai Nomonhan ace who claimed 21 victories whilst flying as the second wingman to the Sentai commander in the Sentai Hombu flight. Promoted to first lieutenant, he later flew in the 2nd Chutai of the 25th Sentai over China, claiming a further five victories. Hosono was killed in action on 6 October 1943 when he deliberately crash-dived his fatally damaged Ki-43 into a river (*Yasuho Izawa*)

flying in the Chutai leader's Shotai. After this early success Takiyama flew as a Shotai leader in all subsequent combat missions that he participated in, raising his score to six victories and five probables. In one desperate fight against superior numbers he managed to shoot down one of his attackers, but not before his Ki-27 was hit 44 times. The fighter turned over on landing but Takiyama survived. Later promoted to major and eventually given command of the 104th Sentai, which was equipped with both the Ki-44 and Ki-84, Takiyama claimed two B-29s shot down for a final score of nine (see *Aircraft of the Aces 100*).

The 3rd Chutai of the 11th Sentai was also in action on 27 June 1939, Sgt Saburo Kimura, in his third combat of the campaign, claiming no fewer than four I-16s and three I-15s in a desperate single-handed fight against eight or nine enemy aircraft. His Ki-27 was hit several times and he was wounded, barely escaping with his life. Kimura returned to the front from hospital on 6 July, despite not having fully recovered, and resumed operational flying the very next day.

In the 4th Chutai, 25-year-old MSgt Takaaki Minami was engaged in a descending dogfight with seven enemy machines, claiming three shot down. He soon found himself at a dangerously low altitude in a badly damaged Ki-27, but luckily for him Sgt Maj Bunji Yoshiyama from the 1st Chutai came to his rescue, allowing Minami to escape home. After Nomonhan, Minami continued to fly the Ki-27 with the 1st Sentai, seeing further combat in the Malayan campaign, in the East Indies and Burma. He eventually claimed 14 victories and survived the war.

Fellow 4th Chutai pilot, and future ace, Cpl Jiro Okuda claimed three Soviet fighters and then returned home with Cpl Naoharu Shiromoto, whose Ki-27 had been hit by ground fire while he was strafing.

With the battle now almost over, the 24th Sentai dropped down looking for stragglers, but with few Soviet aircraft still in the area its pilots busied themselves strafing ground targets instead. WO Kira chased two fleeing I-16s but lost them in a bank of low-lying fog.

Later, a second strike against the more distant airfield at Bain Tumen was flown, requiring the fitting of the unpopular auxiliary fuel tanks to the Ki-27s. There was little aerial opposition to this raid, leaving disappointed fighter pilots to return home anxiously watching their fuel gauges as the weather worsened.

Japanese claims for 27 June were wildly optimistic, with the 11th Sentai claiming 50 victories and three probables, the 1st Sentai 45 victories and three probables and the 24th Sentai three victories. More sanguine staff officers were sceptical about these claims, but the success of the Ki-27 pilots was undoubted, and good for morale. In the initial fighting 70th IAP had lost nine I-16s and five I-15s, with six pilots dead and five wounded, but many more aircraft had been damaged in the air or destroyed on the ground. In 22nd IAP, three I-15s were lost and two returned with wounded pilots, whilst the commander, Maj Kravchenko, had to belly land his I-16. A single I-15 was shot down over Bain Tumen. The 11th Sentai lost two Ki-27s in the fight, with both 1Lt Sadayoshi Mitsutomi and Sgt Maj Kitoshi Hori being killed.

Twenty-year-old Cpl Moritsugi Kanai of the 1st Chutai, 11th Sentai claimed seven victories over Nomonhan as wingman to WO Shinohara. Kanai rose to the rank of first lieutenant and became the leading ace of the 25th Sentai over China, flying the Ki-43 and, later, the Ki-84. He was to eventually claim 26 victories and survive the war, serving in the JSDAF as a major before he was killed in a flying accident in 1972 (*Yasuho Izawa*)

WO Saburo Togo of the 3rd Chutai, 11th Sentai was an experienced pilot of long service who claimed 22 victories over Nomonhan, ranking equal with WO Zenzaburo Ohtsuka as the second-highest scoring ace in the unit (*Yasuho Izawa*)

Lt Gen Giga was reprimanded by Tokyo for his aggressive air offensive into Mongolian territory in the wake of the 27 June missions, and follow-up operations were cancelled due to the onset of bad weather. Action recommenced on 2 July when the JAAF was called upon to support a major Japanese Army offensive against Soviet positions in the high ground of Bain Tsagan, on the western side of the Khalkhin River.

A series of seesaw aerial battles were subsequently fought over the front throughout July as both sides attempted to support troops fighting on the ground. The Soviets employed the relentless 'air conveyor' technique used in Spain to put successive waves of bombers and fighters over the frontline and to the immediate Japanese rear. The JAAF attempted to counter these attacks, but the Ki-27 pilots found themselves engaging one formation after another, often being attacked by new formations when they were themselves at their most vulnerable after their own formations had been broken up in the previous encounter. Additionally, these relentless attacks meant that fighter pilots were required to fly sortie after sortie in an attempt to counter the incursions, exhausting themselves in the process.

On 3 July the 11th Sentai was in action against escorted SB bombers, and Cpl Jiro Okuda of the 4th Chutai claimed one shot down for his fifth victory to make him an ace. This was also one of the first Soviet bombers to be destroyed in the conflict. The next day, during intense aerial fighting involving more than 300 aircraft, Goro Furugori of the 3rd Chutai shot down another SB in a head-on attack, followed by an escorting I-16. He then used his wingtip to cut through the parachute shroud lines of the unfortunate pilot when he bailed out. That evening back at his airfield, Furugori, an accomplished musician, found that one of the strings of his shamisen (a member of the lute family) had been cut.

Sgt Maj Tomio Hanada of the 3rd Chutai claimed three victories to bring his total to six. He then landed to rescue the Chutai leader, Capt Fujita, who had bailed out of his flaming Ki-27 with serious burns. Later that same day the 2nd Chutai of the 24th Sentai attacked another formation of SBs and I-16s, Sgt Maj Koji Ishizawa claiming two fighters before being wounded. He managed to fly back home, and after just two weeks in hospital Ishizawa returned to his unit to continue fighting.

The Japanese pilots believed they were succeeding but many of the I-16s 'shot down' returned safely, in one case with 62 hits to the fuselage and wings and two to the armour plate behind the pilot's seat – proof against the Ki-27's 7.7 mm weapons.

On 5 July two Chutai of the 1st Sentai, led by the Sentai commander Toshio Kato, intercepted a force of 60 SB bombers escorted by 50 I-16s. The JAAF pilots claimed five bombers shot down, which the Soviets admitted, and seven I-16s, which they did not. Sgt Maj Motojima of the 1st Chutai found himself boxed in by ten Soviet fighters after claiming three shot down, but in a succession of increasingly tight turns he managed to extricate himself, claiming another one as he did so to become an ace.

Another 3rd Chutai, 11th Sentai ace was Sgt Maj Goro Furugori, who claimed 20 victories over Nomonhan. After a period serving as an instructor, he added to his score flying the Ki-84 in the 22nd Sentai over China and the Philippines. Sgt Maj Furogori was killed in action over Tacloban on 5 November 1944 in combat with P-38s, eyewitnesses claiming that he had destroyed two Lightnings before being shot down himself (*Yasuho Izawa*)

Five days later WO Mamoru Hanada of the 11th Sentai's 2nd Chutai took off for a sortie without his favourite brown scarf, and in a fight in which he claimed seven I-16s downed – one of them after he had been badly wounded in the leg – he had to force land his damaged Ki-27 within Japanese lines. Hanada's leg was amputated but he died three days later, having accumulated 17 victories in just two weeks.

A Ki-27 Ko of the 1st Sentai is prepared for flight in wet and muddy conditions. The Sentai's insignia consisted of the rudder and elevators painted in the Chutai colours, in this case probably red for the 2nd Chutai. The rudder is marked with the Hiragana character 'Ni', each aircraft being distinguished by an individual character from this alphabet – the 1st Chutai used characters from the katakana alphabet. This aircraft has also had its lower wheel fairings removed, which was a common practice in muddy conditions (*Summer*)

On 12 July, in a clash with 39 I-16s from 22nd IAP and six I-16s and 15 I-15bis of 70th IAP, the 1st Sentai lost two pilots killed and had its commander, Toshio Kato, forced to bail out over enemy territory badly burned. Sgt Toshio Matsuura rescued him, having carried Kato to his aircraft whilst Sgt Majs Tarui and Motojima kept approaching Soviet forces at bay. For this feat Sgt Matsuura was awarded the Order of the Golden Kite 5th Grade. The Soviet fighters had attacked the lower of three stepped formations of Ki-27s, and the subsequent bounce by the remaining two JAAF formations had not shaken them during a 45-minute dogfight over the Khalkhin River. The Japanese pilots claimed 11 victories and admitted three aircraft lost, including Kato's, but only one communist fighter had actually been shot down, its pilot bailing out. The Soviets claimed 11 victories in return.

Sgt Takayori Kodama of the 2nd Chutai, who force-landed that day, recalled;

'I fight well to shoot down 100 aeroplanes, which is my goal. The most desperate fighting until today was that of 12 July. Over Buyr Nuir I found 70 enemy aircraft consisting of I-15s and I-16s, and I fought desperately in a confused battle for 20 minutes against 10+ enemies, receiving 25 hits to my aeroplane. The propeller ceased to turn and, gliding over enemy ground forces, I managed to force land in territory held by friendly troops. I shall, from now on, try to demonstrate my fighting technique.'

On 21 July the 1st and 24th Sentais were in action for nearly 90 minutes against 95 I-16s and 62 I-15bis of 22nd and 70th IAPs. Sgt Maj Shogo Saito claimed four Soviet fighters destroyed and one probable, after which he flew at enemy fighters harrying Lt Shoichi Suzuki (who was flying his first sortie since returning from hospital) even though his guns were inoperable.

Three days later the youngest pilot in the 11th Sentai, Haruo Takagaki, claimed two Soviet aircraft shot down when a formation of SBs, escorted by 35 I-16s from 56th IAP, was bounced on its way back from a bombing mission. These were Takagaki's eighth and ninth claims of an eventual 15 made over Nomonhan. He continued to fly with the 11th over New Guinea, claiming at least two more victories, before joining the 72nd Sentai and seeing further action over the Philippines. Takagaki then returned to Japan to fly with the 246th Sentai, before being posted as a flying instructor to the Kumagaya Flying School. He was killed in a flying accident on 15 July 1945 whilst taking off on a night sortie.

Shogo Saito claimed one of the bombers shot down from a formation of nine on 24 July 1939, but he was wounded by return fire. Despite this he soon resumed combat operations, and by the end of the conflict had

The leading ace of the 3rd Chutai, 11th Sentai was Sgt Maj Tomio Hanada (not to be confused with Mamoru Hanada), who claimed 25 victories over Nomonhan. He was also one of several pilots who landed on the steppe during combat to rescue other pilots. On 4 July 1939, Chutai leader Capt Takashi Fujita, badly burned, had bailed out of his stricken Ki-27. Hanada protected Fujita as he descended by parachute, and then landed to rescue him, both men safely making it back to base. On 7 October 1939 Hanada was killed during a routine training flight at Harbin when his Ki-27 collided with the fighter of Sgt Maj Daisuke Kanbara, the latter managing to save himself by parachute (*Yasuho Izawa*)

claimed 25 victories to make him the highest scoring pilot in the 11th Sentai. He continued to fly the Ki-27 as a warrant officer during the 1942 campaign over the Philippines, and later served with the 78th Sentai over New Guinea after promotion to second lieutenant. Saito, who claimed a B-24 destroyed in a head-on pass in December 1943, was eventually killed in ground combat in New Guinea on 2 July 1944.

One of the biggest encounters of the conflict occurred on 25 July 1939 when the 1st and 11th Sentais fought a total of 118 I-16s from 70th, 22nd and 56th IAPs over the Hamar-Daba heights. Hiromichi Shinohara of the 11th claimed four fighters shot down before his own aircraft was damaged – with fuel streaming from his left wing he was obliged to land. Ten-victory ace Sgt Maj Yutaka Aoyagi immediately landed to pick him up, but his Ki-27 was hit by a round fired from a Soviet tank, leaving him wounded too. Minutes later Sgt Maj Shintaro Kashima's Ki-27 was also hit by a pursuing I-16, forcing the pilot to bail out over the battlefield.

Sgt Maj Koichi Iwase, who had claimed a single victory during the early stages of the engagement, landed with the intention of rescuing Kashima. However, once on the ground he saw that Bunji Yoshiyama, who had claimed three victories a few minutes earlier, had also landed to pick Kashima up. Taking off again, Iwase then saw the battle-damaged Ki-27s of Shinohara and Aoyagi, so he landed once more, again under fire, and rescued both men. For this daring feat Iwase was awarded a citation from the 2nd Hikoshidan commander, Lt Gen Giga.

Iwase eventually claimed ten victories and three probables over Nomonhan, followed by two more kills over China in 1940. After a stint as a flying instructor and recuperation from sickness, he spent most of the Pacific War flying transport aircraft in Japan.

Tomio Hanada of the 11th's 3rd Chutai claimed to have shot down five enemy aircraft on 25 July 1939, although debris from one of his victims seriously damaged his Ki-27. Accumulating a total of 25 victories over Nomonhan, Hanada was killed in a collision with Sgt Maj Daisuke Kanbara during a routine flight over Harbin on 7 October 1939.

The 1st Sentai suffered badly on 25 July 1939, losing 1Lts Koizumi and Honma, whilst 2Lt Chozo Taguchi and Sgt Maj Misao Inoue were both grievously wounded. Inoue eventually recovered, returning to the unit after the conflict had ended. Later in the war he would become the leading ace of the 13th Sentai, flying the twin-engined Kawasaki Ki-45 fighter and the Ki-43 in the western New Guinea theatre and increasing his claims to 16. Inoue was killed on 15 December 1944 in a landing accident whilst at the controls of a Ki-45 from the 5th Sentai.

From 27 July 1939 Soviet fighter regiments started targeting Japanese airfields, low-flying I-16s approaching from 300 ft and then climbing up to 6500 ft, before diving down to make their attacks. On 29 July Capt Saiji Kani and Lt Shoichi Suzuki of the 24th's 1st Chutai were just about to land following a patrol when they were bounced by Soviet fighters low over their landing ground at Alay. Both aces were shot down and killed. At the time of their deaths Kani had claimed nine victories and Suzuki 17. Sgt Maj Jiro Okuda of the 11th Sentai's 4th Chutai was luckier, claiming two Soviet fighters shot down and using his wingtip to slice through the parachute cords of the unfortunate pilot of one of them.

Later that same day the 1st Sentai's CO, Maj Fumio Harada, was taken prisoner after bailing out. The Soviet pilot who had shot him down, Snr Lt V G Rakhov, was later taken to meet Harada at the Japanese pilot's request. After repatriation Maj Harada and the badly burnt 1Lt Naoyuki Daitoku of the 11th Sentai, who had been captured on 6 July, were given pistols and, following a brief 'trial', persuaded by the Kempeitai (Military Police) to commit suicide.

Ki-27s of the 1st Sentai at Saienjo. In the foreground is the oft-depicted Ki-27 of the 1st Chutai leader, Capt Shigetoshi Inoue, with katakana character 'Na' on the rudder, and behind it is the aircraft of Cpl Miyoshi Shimamura. Although the chevron on the forward fuselage of Inoue's Ki-27 is usually depicted in artwork as white, it is the author's belief that it was possibly yellow (*Kenji Takeyoshi via Yasuho Izawa*)

AUGUST ATTRITION

On 4 August, whilst engaging I-16s of 22nd IAP returning from raids against Japanese airfields, future ace Goro Nishihara of the 24th Sentai rescued Lt Col Kojiro Matsumura, who had been forced down in enemy territory in a burning Ki-27. Nishihara, braving Soviet tank and machine gun fire, landed alongside the badly burned and now unconscious Matsumura and extricated him from his fighter. With his CO safely aboard his Ki-27, Nishihara took off and headed home. Sixteen-victory ace Muneyoshi Motojima of the 1st Sentai's 1st Chutai was not so fortunate, however, being shot down and killed during the dogfight.

Twelve-victory ace Tokuyaso Ishizuka of the 11th's 2nd Chutai fell victim to Soviet fighters the following day when his Ki-27 was deliberately rammed by an I-16 flown by Lt Aleksandr Moshin. Miraculously thrown clear of his shattered machine by the impact, he had time to use his parachute and descend into hostile territory. After evading Soviet forces for three days, Ishizuka was finally found exhausted on the 9th by a Japanese patrol, having crossed the Khalka River to safety. In Japanese reports the incident was referred to as a collision with an I-15bis, but according to Moshin he pursued Ishizuka down to low level and then, having run out of ammunition, he deliberately sawed off the Ki-27's tailplanes and rudder with his propeller.

5 August also saw ace Taro Kobayashi resort to ramming to claim a victory, although it cost him his life. Engaging ten SBs escorted by 15 I-153s, Kobayashi was reported to have shot down two Soviet fighters before he deliberately rammed a third. This trio of victories took his final tally to ten.

Two days later, yet another attempt by Soviet fighters to attack Japanese landing grounds was intercepted by 11th Sentai Ki-27s. Nineteen-victory ace Saburo Kimura of the 3rd Chutai was badly wounded in the left thigh shortly after downing an I-16, and when he attempted to land his Ki-27 at Uzursui airfield the fighter somersaulted and he received further injuries. He died the following day.

The intensity of the fighting on 7 August was demonstrated when seven-victory ace Daisuke Kanbara from the 11th Sentai landed close to a Soviet pilot who had bailed out of a fighter that he had just shot down and duly killed him with his sword. Despite these much publicised

Capt Takejiro Koyanagi and his 1st Sentai Ki-27, marked with the Hiragana character 'A' on its rudder and red lightning bolt command stripes on its wings. Capt Koyanagi was the 2nd Chutai leader. Note the rearview mirror attached to the windscreen and the cord dangling from the cockpit. The latter could simply be to assist entry, or more likely in this case the radio lead for the pilot's headset (*Kyushichi Noguchi via Yasuho Izawa*)

demonstrations of martial determination, the gradual attrition of experienced Ki-27 pilots was to continue.

On 12 August, after a lull in the action due to bad weather, the JAAF attempted to reverse the defensive posture imposed on it by carrying the fight to the enemy. This new tactic saw Ki-27 units venturing across the Khalka River in formations consisting of one or two Chutais. They were gradually overwhelmed, however, by successive formations of I-16s totalling 137 aircraft. Sgt Maj Masao Ashida of the 11th Sentai's 3rd Chutai was flying his third sortie of the day when his unit engaged a formation of nine I-16s. After shooting down one of the Soviet machines, his own aircraft was fatally damaged and he was seen to ram another, before plunging to his death. That final act took Ashida's score to 13 victories. That same day, in a battle against overwhelming odds, Jiro Okuda of the 11th Sentai's 4th Chutai was also killed moments after downing his 14th opponent.

In response to the increasing losses, the 64th Sentai arrived at the front on 15 August 1939, taking up residence on a makeshift airfield called Hoshiu, north of Uzur Nuir. After an uneventful patrol on the 17th, the Sentai's airfield was strafed by Soviet fighters on 19 August, resulting in one Ki-27 being destroyed. On the 20th – the day a major Soviet ground offensive was launched – five 64th Sentai Ki-27s out on patrol encountered I-16s, claiming four of them shot down. Later that same day there was another dogfight with a much larger enemy formation, during which future ace Sgt Maj Tokuya Sudo, in Lt Sakai's Shotai, shot down one of the ten victories claimed by the Sentai.

Shortly after the 64th Sentai completed its fifth sortie of 20 August more than 70 Soviet fighters strafed Hoshiu, damaging 17 of the unit's Ki-27s, six of them significantly. After this attack the 64th withdrew to Saienjo airfield.

That same day the 1st and 11th Sentais were also in action. After damaging an I-16, ace Bunji Yoshiyama of the 11th Sentai's 1st Chutai ran out of ammunition, but he continued to chase the Soviet fighter with the intention of ramming it. When his opponent hastily crash-landed on the steppe, Yoshiyama landed beside the damaged I-16 and shot the Soviet pilot dead with his pistol. He then relieved his victim of his sidearm and wristwatch as grisly souvenirs.

On 21 August the JAAF launched Operation 'S' – a long-planned second air offensive intended to destroy Soviet aircraft on their airfields at Tamsag Bulag. Lt Gen Giga committed 70 per cent of his fighting strength in Manchuria in order to ensure the campaign's success. After a series of preliminary early morning strikes by light bombers, the main wave of 24 light bombers, 12 heavy bombers and 15 close support aircraft, escorted by 88 Ki-27s from the 1st, 11th and 64th Sentais, commenced their attack. In the air combats that followed, the Ki-27 units claimed 54 victories and eight probables, whilst admitting (*text continues on page 46*)

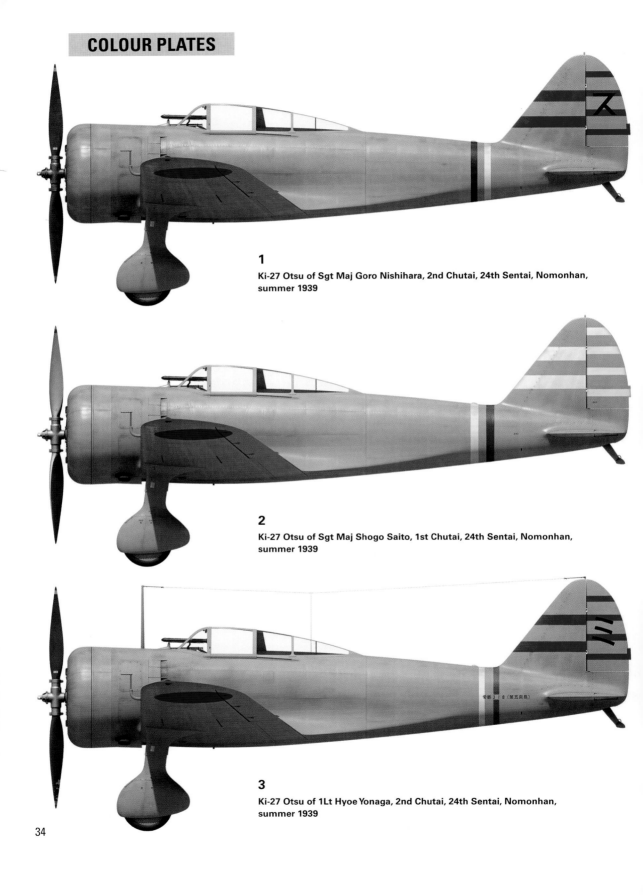

1
Ki-27 Otsu of Sgt Maj Goro Nishihara, 2nd Chutai, 24th Sentai, Nomonhan, summer 1939

2
Ki-27 Otsu of Sgt Maj Shogo Saito, 1st Chutai, 24th Sentai, Nomonhan, summer 1939

3
Ki-27 Otsu of 1Lt Hyoe Yonaga, 2nd Chutai, 24th Sentai, Nomonhan, summer 1939

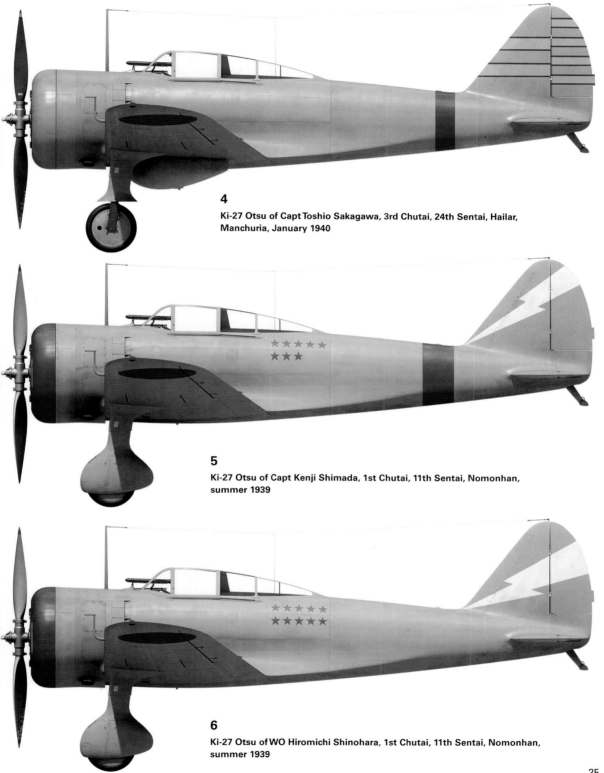

4
Ki-27 Otsu of Capt Toshio Sakagawa, 3rd Chutai, 24th Sentai, Hailar, Manchuria, January 1940

5
Ki-27 Otsu of Capt Kenji Shimada, 1st Chutai, 11th Sentai, Nomonhan, summer 1939

6
Ki-27 Otsu of WO Hiromichi Shinohara, 1st Chutai, 11th Sentai, Nomonhan, summer 1939

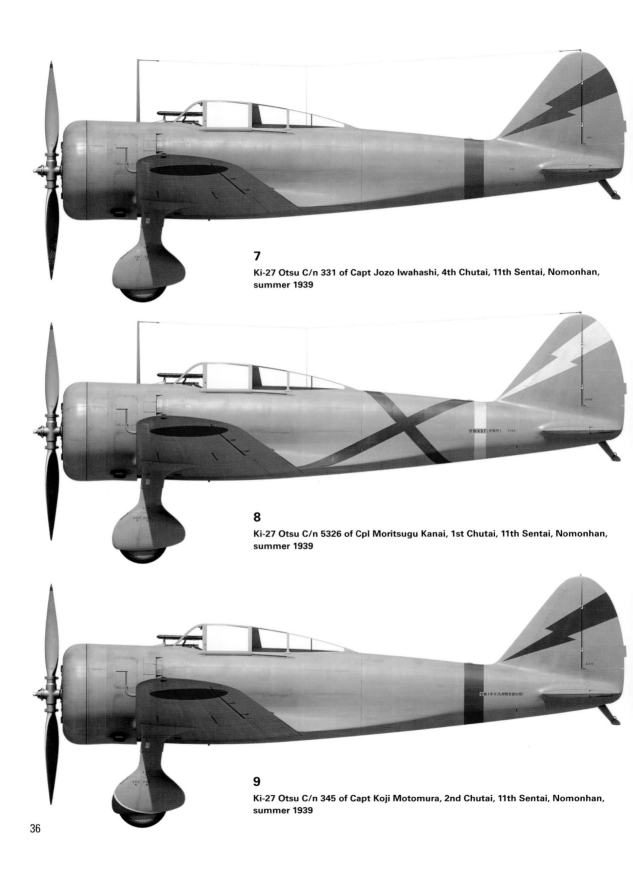

7
Ki-27 Otsu C/n 331 of Capt Jozo Iwahashi, 4th Chutai, 11th Sentai, Nomonhan, summer 1939

8
Ki-27 Otsu C/n 5326 of Cpl Moritsugu Kanai, 1st Chutai, 11th Sentai, Nomonhan, summer 1939

9
Ki-27 Otsu C/n 345 of Capt Koji Motomura, 2nd Chutai, 11th Sentai, Nomonhan, summer 1939

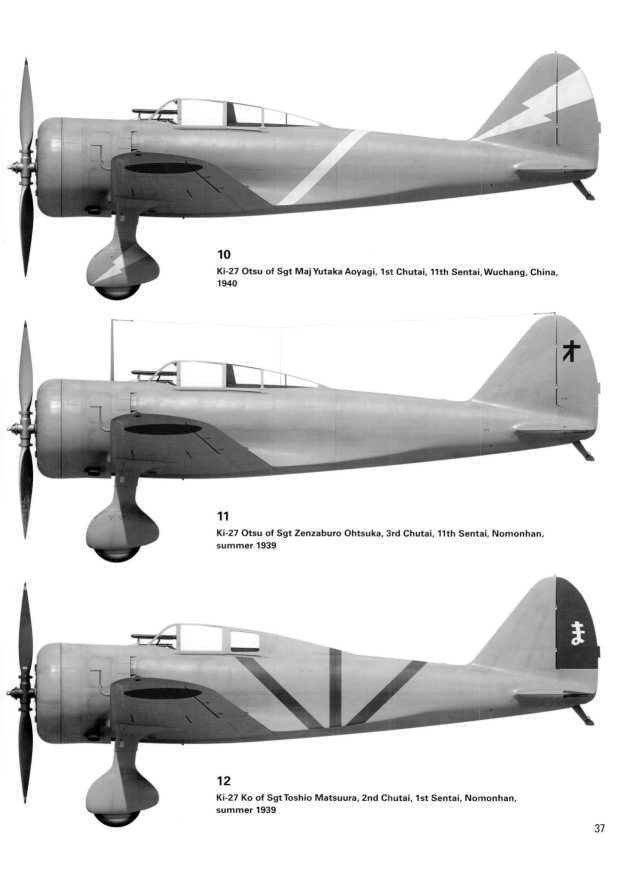

10
Ki-27 Otsu of Sgt Maj Yutaka Aoyagi, 1st Chutai, 11th Sentai, Wuchang, China,
1940

11
Ki-27 Otsu of Sgt Zenzaburo Ohtsuka, 3rd Chutai, 11th Sentai, Nomonhan,
summer 1939

12
Ki-27 Ko of Sgt Toshio Matsuura, 2nd Chutai, 1st Sentai, Nomonhan,
summer 1939

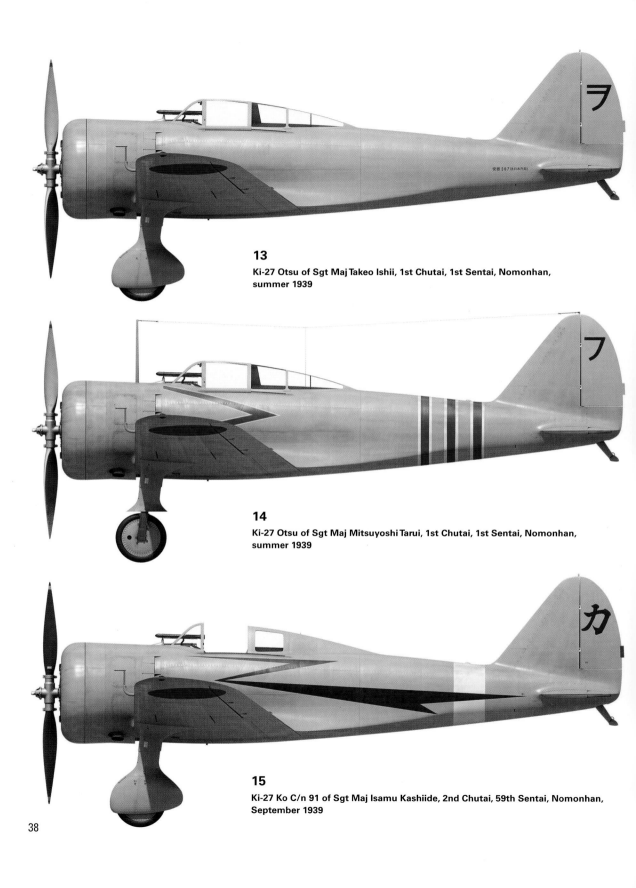

13
Ki-27 Otsu of Sgt Maj Takeo Ishii, 1st Chutai, 1st Sentai, Nomonhan,
summer 1939

14
Ki-27 Otsu of Sgt Maj Mitsuyoshi Tarui, 1st Chutai, 1st Sentai, Nomonhan,
summer 1939

15
Ki-27 Ko C/n 91 of Sgt Maj Isamu Kashiide, 2nd Chutai, 59th Sentai, Nomonhan,
September 1939

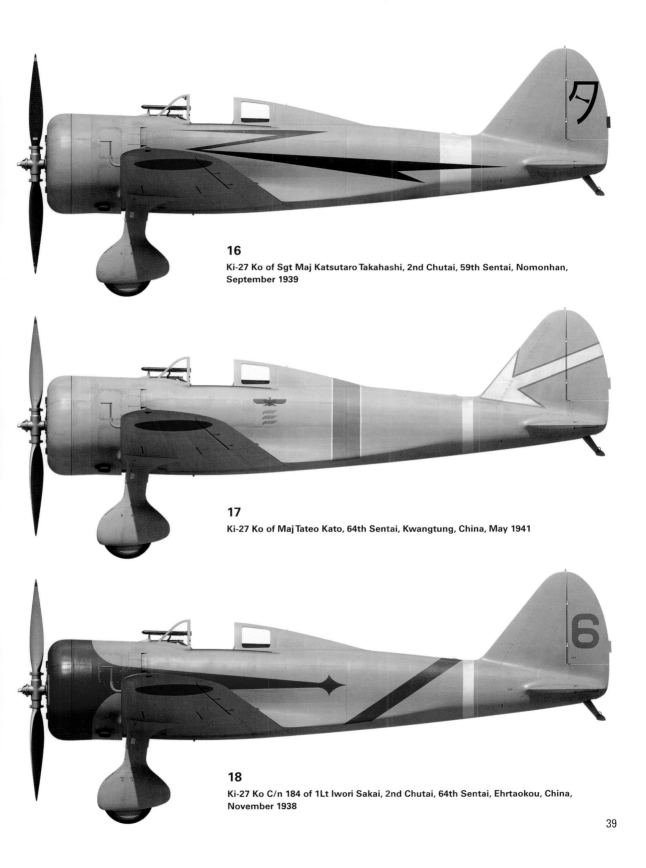

16
Ki-27 Ko of Sgt Maj Katsutaro Takahashi, 2nd Chutai, 59th Sentai, Nomonhan,
September 1939

17
Ki-27 Ko of Maj Tateo Kato, 64th Sentai, Kwangtung, China, May 1941

18
Ki-27 Ko C/n 184 of 1Lt Iwori Sakai, 2nd Chutai, 64th Sentai, Ehrtaokou, China,
November 1938

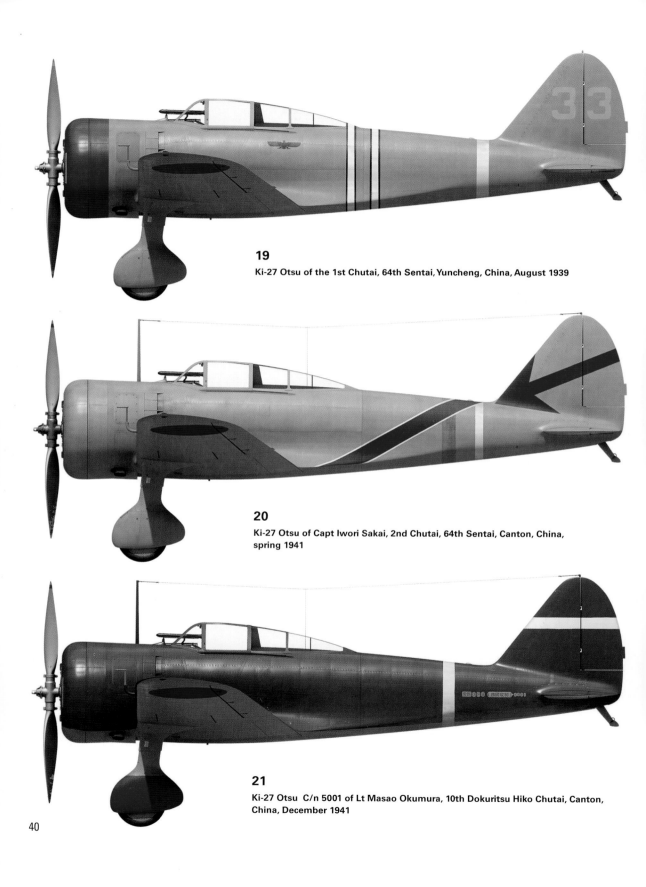

19
Ki-27 Otsu of the 1st Chutai, 64th Sentai, Yuncheng, China, August 1939

20
Ki-27 Otsu of Capt Iwori Sakai, 2nd Chutai, 64th Sentai, Canton, China,
spring 1941

21
Ki-27 Otsu C/n 5001 of Lt Masao Okumura, 10th Dokuritsu Hiko Chutai, Canton,
China, December 1941

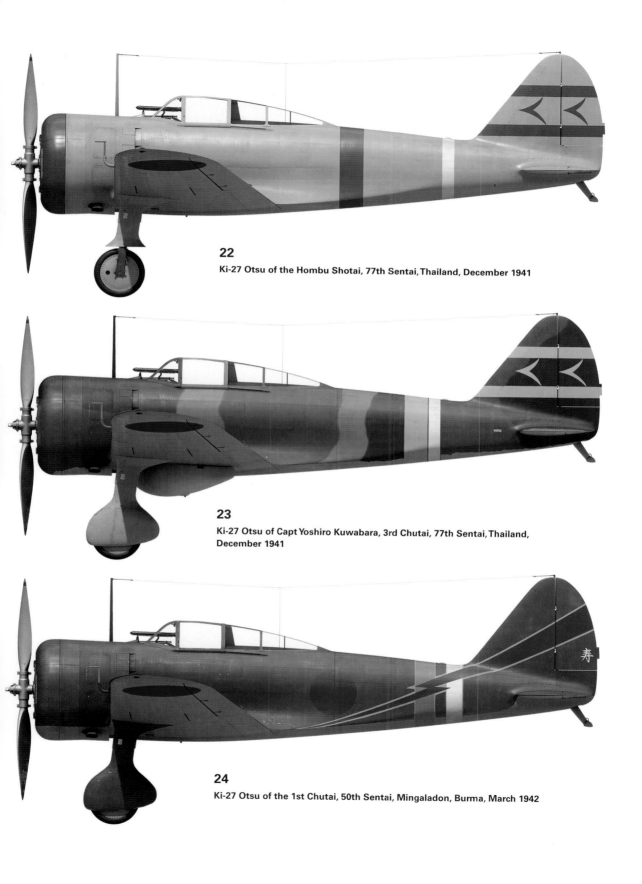

22
Ki-27 Otsu of the Hombu Shotai, 77th Sentai, Thailand, December 1941

23
Ki-27 Otsu of Capt Yoshiro Kuwabara, 3rd Chutai, 77th Sentai, Thailand,
December 1941

24
Ki-27 Otsu of the 1st Chutai, 50th Sentai, Mingaladon, Burma, March 1942

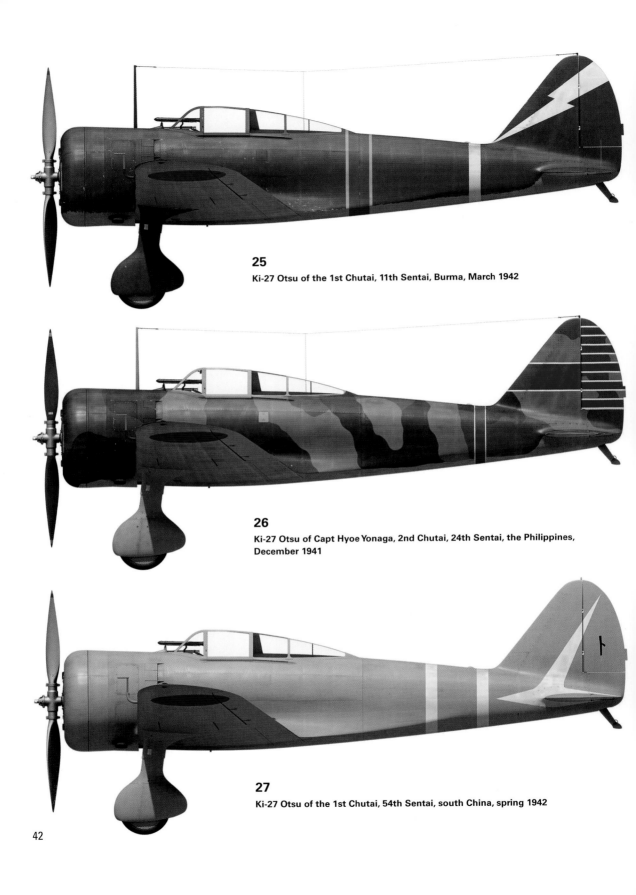

25
Ki-27 Otsu of the 1st Chutai, 11th Sentai, Burma, March 1942

26
Ki-27 Otsu of Capt Hyoe Yonaga, 2nd Chutai, 24th Sentai, the Philippines,
December 1941

27
Ki-27 Otsu of the 1st Chutai, 54th Sentai, south China, spring 1942

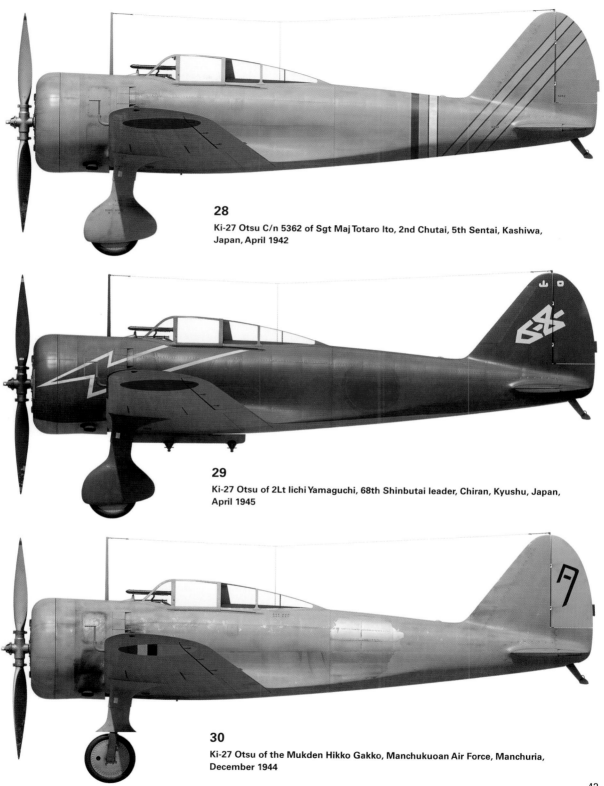

28
Ki-27 Otsu C/n 5362 of Sgt Maj Totaro Ito, 2nd Chutai, 5th Sentai, Kashiwa,
Japan, April 1942

29
Ki-27 Otsu of 2Lt Iichi Yamaguchi, 68th Shinbutai leader, Chiran, Kyushu, Japan,
April 1945

30
Ki-27 Otsu of the Mukden Hikko Gakko, Manchukuoan Air Force, Manchuria,
December 1944

31 (above and right)
Ki-27 Otsu of Capt Shigetoshi Inoue, 1st Chutai, 1st Sentai, Saienjo,
Manchuria, 1939

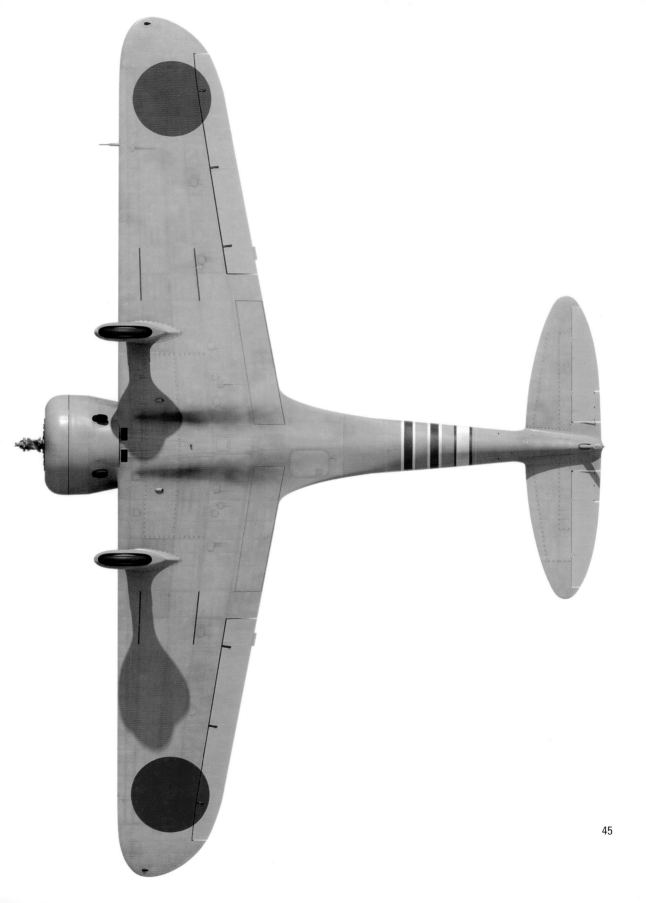

the loss of four fighters and their pilots (three from the 64th), although several wounded pilots and damaged aircraft that returned would never fly in combat again.

One of the latter was 18-victory ace Sgt Maj Takeo Ishii of the 1st Sentai's 1st Chutai. Grievously wounded when his aircraft was hit 60 times, he managed to return to his landing ground and was subsequently hospitalised for two years. Ishii eventually returned to flying as an instructor at the Kumagaya and Tachiarai Flying Schools, spending the last year of the war teaching student pilots to become suicide attackers.

2Lt Katsumi Anma of the 64th, later to become a noted ace in the Ki-43 over Burma, also returned home with his Ki-27 badly shot up after claiming a victory on 21 August.

The following day the 11th Sentai's 2nd Chutai leader, Capt Koji Motomura, who had claimed 14 victories over Nomonhan, was shot down and killed.

On 24 August Yoshihiko Yajima of the 2nd Chutai of the 1st Sentai wrote in his diary;

'Escorts to bombers, took off 1350 hrs. Score – one destroyed and two probables, but Capt Masuda failed to return. I think that of the officer pilots who left Kagamigahara only Yajima remains, and now I have lost my new Chutai leader. Lost – two Sentai commanders, two Chutai leaders and all the officer pilots. Why do only I live through it all? Shame on me, shame on me! I must die 10,000 times for this sin!'

The very next day Yajima was killed whilst escorting bombers, having claimed a total of 16 victories in more than 90 sorties. Aircraft from the 64th Sentai were flying alongside the 1st Sentai on this mission, and the unit lost three pilots including its CO, Maj Hachio Yokoyama. Found by Manchurian cavalry, he had suffered such severe injuries that he had to have both his arms amputated. The Sentai's executive officer, Capt Seizo Okuyama, had bailed out, and he returned to the unit two days later to assume command, but Sgt Maj Matsuzo Kasai was killed.

The 11th Sentai's 11-victory ace Eisaku Suzuki was also lost on 25 August when he was bounced at the end of a patrol by an I-153 from 22nd IAP.

Despite these growing losses, not all the Ki-27 pilots were becoming demoralised. WO Tokuya Sudo of the 64th's 2nd Chutai wrote the following entry in his diary on 28 August in reference to a diving-and-zooming fight he had had the previous day;

'The situation [here] is very different from that in China, and it's worth doing, for the enemy's fighting tactics are different and I am also learning a lot.'

That evening the ranking ace of the JAAF, WO Hiromichi Shinohara of the 11th Sentai, was shot down and killed after reportedly destroying three aircraft to take his score to 58. He had been escorting a bomber formation when it was attacked by I-16s, and in the swirling dogfight that followed he was struck from behind by fire from a Soviet fighter and lost control of his Ki-27. His wingman, Sgt Maj Ohno, had watched helplessly, unable to intervene as the ace's fighter fell in flames into Mohoheri Lake.

The leading ace of the Nomonhan conflict was another pilot of the 11th Sentai, Sgt Maj Hiromichi Shinohara, who claimed 58 victories as a member of Capt Shimada's 1st Chutai. He kept a detailed score of his victories in his diary, insisting that only aircraft seen to fall in flames were counted. Exactly four months after his first air combat Shinohara was shot down and killed on 27 August 1939 (*Yasuho Izawa*)

SEPTEMBER SWANSONG

The 64th Sentai continued to fight over Nomonhan until the end of the conflict, claiming 52 victories for the loss of eight pilots. Although several pilots from the Sentai went on to become aces in later campaigns, none became exclusively Ki-27 aces over Nomonhan. The 64th's highest scoring pilots were Sgt Maj Tokuya Sudo, who claimed at least four victories, including two shared, to bring his overall tally to ten, and Hiroshi Sekiguchi, who added four claims over Nomonhan to his single shared success against the Chinese whilst flying the Ki-10. Sgt Maj Sudo was shot down and killed on 1 September immediately after scoring his tenth victory. He was one of four 64th Sentai pilots lost that day, as was the 2nd Chutai leader Capt Shuichi Anzai.

The 1st Sentai's 11-victory ace Sgt Takayori Kodama, who had been flying as wingman to the acting Sentai commander and executive officer, Capt Yasuo Makino, was also shot down and killed on 1 September. He had failed to reach his goal of 100 victories that he had promised himself in July.

Following the death of Capt Anzai, Lt Iwori Sakai was appointed to lead the 2nd Chutai of the 64th Sentai. By now the strain of several months of constant combat was being felt, as he recalled. 'I had to fly four to six missions a day, and I was so greatly fatigued that often I could barely see to land my aeroplane. The enemy aeroplanes came over like a black cloud, and our losses were very heavy'. So tired were the 64th's pilots that they were no longer able to eat the steaks prepared for them by the airfield battalion's cook, who had been a chef at a top class hotel in Yokohama before the conflict. Sakai believed that the unit had lost two-thirds of its strength in its first month of operations.

On 15 September, in a final fling against the Soviet airfields, the whole Ki-27 force and two light bomber Sentais crossed the river. Two Chutais (totalling 20 Ki-27s) from the newly arrived 59th Sentai were intercepted by 50 Soviet fighters, and 11 of the communist aircraft were claimed to have been shot down. The 59th's 1st Chutai then pursued the surviving Polikarpovs, only to be bounced by another Soviet formation. Six Ki-27s and their pilots, including the Chutai leader, Capt Mitsugu Yamamoto, were lost.

Four 59th Sentai pilots emerged from this fight with two victory claims apiece, and they would go on to become aces during World War 2 – Yasuhiko Kuroe with 30 victories (see *Aircraft of the Aces 13, 85* and *100* for more details), Katsutaro Takahashi with 13 victories and Takeomi

A splendid image of a Ki-27 Ko of the 59th Sentai flying in a cloudy sky. The Ko was the earliest operational model of the Ki-27, and it was distinguished by the solid rear canopy fairing with rectangular windows on either side behind the pilot. Here, the pilot flies with the centre canopy section removed from the aircraft – a common practice. The lightning bolt on the fuselage is the Sentai insignia, painted in the Chutai colours, although the sequence and colours are disputed. The katakana character on the rudder is 'O' (Oh). The 59th joined the fighting over Nomonhan too late for any of its pilots to become aces, but some of them were to distinguish themselves later, including Maj Yasuhiko Kuroe with 30 claimed victories in various units (*Summer*)

Hayashi and Isamu Kashiide with nine victories each.

On this very last day of fighting in the Nomonhan Conflict, 27-victory ace Kenji Shimada and his wingman 20-victory ace Bunji Yoshiyama, both from the 11th Sentai, failed to return from an engagement with a superior force of I-16s. It is presumed that they were shot down and killed.

A truce came into effect on 16 September 1939, thus bringing the war to an end. Despite the losses, and the exhaustion suffered by its pilots, the Ki-27 had held up well in a situation where Soviet air power had escalated from just over 100 aircraft to around 600, whilst the number of Japanese machines remained less than half that. In addition, the quality of Soviet pilots, and their tactics, had steadily improved as the conflict ground on. The JAAF admitted that it had lost 63 fighters in air combat, with a further 157 being damaged and subsequently repaired. A total of 64 Japanese fighter pilots had been reported as killed, but some captured aviators, and others who committed suicide when forced down in enemy territory, were not reported as combat fatalities. Soviet fighter regiments claimed that they had lost 130 aircraft.

Sgt Maj Isamu Kashiide, seen here in an image that provides a fine view of the Ki-27's radiator and propeller, was another 59th Sentai pilot who distinguished himself after the Nomonhan fighting, having claimed two victories late in that conflict. He later became the leading B-29 hunter in the 4th Sentai over Japan, flying the twin-engined Ki-45 Toryu, eventually claiming seven of the bombers. Kashiide survived the war with the rank of captain, having become a Bukosho winner

Sgt Maj Kashiide's Ki-27 Ko of the 2nd Chutai, 59th Sentai, with the katakana character 'Ka' on the rudder (*Isamu Kashiide via Yasuho Izawa*)

ACTION OVER THE PHILIPPINES

The JAAF fighter strength deployed during the invasion of the Philippines in December 1941 was relatively modest, consisting of only two Ki-27-equipped Sentais. Both units came under the command of the 5th Hikoshidan on Formosa and had a nominal strength of 36 aircraft each. The 24th Sentai, led by Maj Takahashi Takeshi, was an experienced unit from the Nomonhan fighting based at Heito and Choshu. The 50th Sentai, commanded by Maj Makino Yasuo, was a more recent creation, having been formed with two Chutais in September 1940 from the expansion of the fighter Chutai of the 8th Hiko Rentai. It had then been increased in size to full Sentai status with three Chutais in August 1941. The 50th was based at Koshun, and many of its pilots were recently graduated NCOs, including one by the name of Satoshi Anabuki, who was destined for fame.

When the offensive commenced on 8 December 1941, both Sentais sortied aircraft to provide convoy protection for vessels of the Tanaka and Kanno Shitais (task forces), then approaching the northern Philippines. The 24th Sentai completed 25 sorties and the 50th 22. The following day the 24th sent a detachment to operate from Basco airfield on recently captured Batan Island, situated halfway between Formosa and the northern tip of the Philippines. That evening, 5th Hikoshidan Operation Order No 136 instructed the 24th Sentai to support the landings of the Kanno Shitai at Vigan, on the northwestern coast of Luzon. In the event that Vigan airfield was captured following the invasion, the Sentai was to send a detachment there. The 50th Sentai, meanwhile, was to cover the Tanaka Shitai landings at Aparri, on the northern Luzon coast.

On 10 December pilots from the 24th Sentai had their first taste of combat against their new American foes when six Ki-27s patrolling over the landings at Vigan encountered five P-40s, claiming one shot down. They also observed, but did not intercept, two B-17D Flying Fortresses from the 14th Bomb Squadron (BS) flown by 1Lt Guilford Montgomery (40-3086) and Capt Elmer Parsel (40-3074). Later that same day the 50th Sentai despatched Ki-27s to strafe ground targets of opportunity on the Aparri-Tuguegaro road. During the course of this mission 2Lt Teizu Kanamaru's section of four fighters encountered the 14th BS B-17D of 1Lt George E Schaetzel (40-3091), which had just bombed the Japanese landings.

Ki-27 Otsu of the 50th Sentai in the Philippines. The distinctive lightning bolt – the Sentai emblem – was painted in the Chutai colour, and each aircraft 'named' with one or two kanji characters painted on the rudder. Generally, the characters assigned were for types of bird in the 1st Chutai (e.g. 'eagle'), moral exhortations in the 2nd Chutai (e.g. 'loyalty') and types of winds in the 3rd Chutai (e.g. 'imperial wind'), but there were exceptions to this. The 50th was unusual in displaying the national insignia – the hinomaru (the sun's red disc) – on the fuselage before this became common practice on fighters of the JAAF towards the end of 1942 (*Mohei Tokada via Yasuho Izawa*)

After claiming four enemy bombers shot down over China whilst serving as a corporal in the 10th DHC, Teizo Kanamaru had been admitted to the Army Flying Academy in December 1940 and had graduated in July 1941, before being posted to the 50th Sentai's third Chutai. His wingman on 10 December 1941 was Cpl Satoshi Anabuki, the 20-year-old son of a farmer just commencing his distinguished career as a Ki-27 fighter pilot. Anabuki would go on to claim a total of 39 victories, thus making him the second ranking JAAF ace and earning him both an individual citation and the nickname 'Momotaro of Burma'. The latter title was a reference to the folk-tale conqueror of Onigashima (Island of Ogres), a pugnacious warrior-child who during the war became the central character of many cartoon propaganda films.

Also flying in Kanamaru's Shotai on 10 December 1941 was yet another 20-year-old pilot destined to 'make ace', Isamu Sasaki. He had joined the Sentai just before the outbreak of war. Anabuki, Sasaki and Yukio Shimokawa would earn themselves the sobriquet the 'Three Musketeers' of the 50th Sentai over Burma. By April 1944, when he was posted to the Army Test Centre in Japan, 'Skilled Sasaki' had claimed a total of 32 aircraft shot down over Burma. Flying a variety of experimental fighters in his new role as a test pilot, Sasaki claimed six B-29s shot down and three damaged whilst with the test centre. Awarded a promotion as well as the Bukosho in July 1945, he survived the war with a total of 38 victories to his name.

The four Ki-27 pilots set about 1Lt Schaetzel's B-17D like hounds harrying a bull, riddling its wing and one of its engines. 2Lt Kanamaru claimed that he had shot the bomber down, but the Flying Fortress managed to escape into cloud with a ruptured oil tank and landed safely at San Marcelino with the crew unscathed.

After attacking Schaetzel's bomber, 2Lt Kanamaru spotted another B-17 that was being flown by Lt Earl R Tash to Clark Field for repair. The gunners aboard the Flying Fortress responded vigorously to the attacking runs made by the Ki-27, despite SSgt M Bibin receiving serious wounds. Pfc A E Norgaard claimed one of the Japanese fighters shot down, his victim almost certainly being 2Lt Kanamaru, whose fighter received hits to its engine. Forced to abandon the attack, Kanamaru made a forced landing on Colayan Island. Nevertheless, he claimed, erroneously, that he had shot down Tash's B-17 for his sixth kill.

The Japanese viewed the B-17 as 'a tough and well-armed adversary, and one that was very difficult to shoot down. It could absorb an incredible amount of damage and still remain airborne'. At the time it was considered a heroic accomplishment for a Ki-27 'David', with its two rifle-calibre machine guns, to bring down a Flying Fortress 'Goliath'.

After this fight the three remaining 50th Sentai Ki-27s landed at Aparri airfield, which had just been captured.

Bad weather on 11 December limited 24th Sentai operations to Combat Air Patrols (CAPs) over Vigan

1Lt Teizo Kanamaru was a Shotai leader in the 3rd Chutai of the 50th Sentai who had previously claimed four victories over China in the 10th DHC. During the invasion of the Philippines he made claims for two B-17s destroyed, although in reality they were only damaged. Kanamaru was also credited with a P-40 kill. Flying in his Shotai at this time were three other future aces, Satoshi Anabuki, Isamu Sasaki and Yukio Shimokawa. Lt Kanamaru was killed by a bomb on 24 December 1942 whilst attempting to take off from Magwe, Burma, during an RAF night raid (*Yasuho Izawa*)

Sgt Isamu 'Skilled' Sasaki was one of the 'Three Musketeers' of the 50th Sentai, with Satoshi Anabuki and Yukio Shimakawa. Although he flew in Lt Kanamaru's Shotai over the Philippines, he scored his first victory over Burma in early 1942. Sasaki served in Burma with the 50th for more than two years, claiming 32 victories before being posted to the Army Flight Test Centre in Japan. Here, he continued to fly air defence sorties against the B-29 raids, claiming six bombers shot down and three damaged. These successes earned Sasaki the Bukosho award, and promotion to warrant officer. Having survived the conflict, Sasaki served post-war in the JSDAF, reaching the rank of major (*Yasujo Izawa*)

whilst the balance of the Sentai – 18 aircraft – redeployed from Choshu to Vigan airfield. That evening the 5th Hikoshidan issued Operational Order No 139 instructing the 50th Sentai to redeploy from Koshun, on Formosa, to Aparri airfield and then to move on to Vigan on 15-16 December. Whilst at Aparri the following day the 50th lost two of its fighters to the 17th Pursuit Squadron's CO, 1Lt Boyd 'Buzz' Wagner, during his famous strafing run – he actually claimed four Ki-27s shot down over the airfield in his P-40E.

From 13 December both Ki-27 units began a series of fruitless attacks against Del Carmen, Cabanatuan and Clark airfields with small sections of aircraft, whilst two fighters from the 50th Sentai that were on CAP over Aparri encountered the 17th PS P-40E of 1Lt Walt Coss on a reconnaissance mission. Coss had dropped out of the overcast over Aparri to find himself below and in front of the two patrolling Ki-27s, positioning them perfectly for an attack – one of them promptly shot him down. Coss managed to bail out, survived being strafed on the ground by the Ki-27s and then made a dangerous hike to safety.

On 20 December six Ki-27s of the 24th Sentai, flying a sweep to Nichols Field, shot down the P-35A of 17th PS pilot 1Lt Steve Crosby who was returning to Clark Field after a ground attack mission. Crosby had managed to loop his P-35 onto the tail of one of his foes, but he was then shot down by the wingman. The Japanese pilot's fire smashed his instrument panel and severed oil and fuel lines, 'causing a bright tongue of flame to blow back into the cockpit'. Crosby abandoned his burning aircraft very close to the ground but survived the bail out.

One of the notable Ki-27 pilots in the 24th at this time was Nomonhan veteran Sgt Maj (later WO) Koji Oshizawa, who claimed 11+ victories overall.

During the morning of 22 December the 50th Sentai's 3rd Chutai, patrolling over Lingayen Gulf, intercepted six P-40Es of the 17th PS that were attacking Japanese shipping laying offshore. Cpl Anabuki claimed one of the American fighters shot down in this fight as his first victory. Lt Boyd Wagner had just completed a strafing run on a cruiser and minesweeper when he was bounced by Ki-27s whose fire smashed through his windscreen, one of the bullets hitting his left shoulder. Despite his eyes being peppered with glass and metal fragments, Wagner managed to join up with two other P-40s and escape.

A second P-40 pilot, Lt William 'Red' Shepherd, was chased by a Ki-27 that put more than 200 holes in his aircraft before he managed to evade it by 'steep dives, high G-turns and a "sloppy Immelmann" into the overcast'. After this encounter Shepherd made a second attack on the Japanese warships in his damaged P-40, before returning to Clark with an overheating engine that failed on approach, forcing him to make a dead stick landing. His damaged fighter was written off.

Another P-40 pilot had been pursued by at least seven Ki-27s before encountering more of them at a higher altitude and eventually escaping into the mountains with the Japanese fighters 'all about him'. Two Japanese pilots – 1Lt Iguro Yoshihisa and 2Lt Tasumitsu Wada – from the 50th

A Ki-27 Otsu is prepared for operations. This photograph reveals how the vulnerable annular oil cooler sat slightly proud of the front of the engine cowling, and also how the undercarriage struts protruded above the top surface of the wings when the oleos were compressed. This image shows to advantage the optical, telescopic gunsight common to all models of the Ki-27. The white rubber pad at its rear allowed the pilot to put his eye to the sight whilst flying, although this impeded situational awareness during firing. When not in use the sight was protected by a streamlined cap, shown here in place, which could be opened by the operating rod beneath the tube of the sight. The arrangement of access panels and cooling flaps on the cowling can also be appreciated. The small window to the rear of the flaps provided illumination and a visual check on the state of the machine guns, which were fitted to the cockpit floor just below it. The magazines were loaded from beneath the aircraft through panels in the centre section (*Summer*)

Sentai were reported missing after this engagement, although it appears that no American pilots made claims for Ki-27s shot down.

Four days later, on 26 December, another P-40 reconnaissance mission over the Lamon area resulted in 2Lt George Kiser of the 17th PS claiming to have shot down a Type 96 Mitsubishi 'Claude' (an IJNAF monoplane fighter with a spatted undercarriage similar to the Ki-27 in appearance). His victim just might have been the leader of the 24th Sentai's 3rd Chutai, Capt Hinotsume Hyosuke, who was reported killed that day, but as a result of a flying accident. The 26th also saw Capt Charles 'Bud' Sprague and Lt Ed Dyess (CO of the 21st PS) bounced by five Ki-27s whilst returning to their secret airfield at Lubao following a reconnaissance flight over Lingayen. The encounter was inconclusive and the Americans were able to evade the Japanese fighters.

The 50th Sentai claimed two P-40s shot down over Lingayen on 27 December, but these victories cannot be reconciled with any admitted American losses. It is almost certain that the claims actually occurred the following day when 1Lt William Dyess and a wingman were bounced by Ki-27s whilst on another reconnaissance mission over Lingayen. Lt Dyess' wingman had disappeared during this attack and was not seen again, but Lt Dyess engaged a Ki-27 that had surprised him from behind and below. After receiving hits Dyess rolled into a dive and zoom climbed up behind the Ki-27. The Japanese fighter turned into him with ease, and both aircraft attacked each other head on. Dyess claimed that he shot away the top of the Ki-27's engine and saw it descend in flames. He then managed to get back to Lubao with 27 bullet holes in his P-40.

The 24th Sentai was re-deployed back to Kwangtung Army control at Yamentun, near Tsisihar in Manchuria, on 7 January 1942. That same day the 5th Hikoshidan, with the 1st and 2nd Chutai of the 50th Sentai, was re-deployed to Thailand, via Formosa, the unit being tasked with reinforcing the air campaign in Burma, which was proving more difficult than expected (see Chapter 4). The 3rd Chutai of the 50th, equipped with 11 Ki-27s, was to remain in the Philippines under 14th Army control as part of the 10th Dokuritsu Hikotai (Independent Air Group), commanded by Col Hoshi Kametaro.

Satoshi Anabuki forged his flying career over the Philippines as a 19-year-old corporal in Lt Kanamaru's Shotai of the 3rd Chutai, 50th Sentai, where he claimed three P-40s. Anabuki continued to fly with the 50th, acquiring the nickname 'Momotaro of Burma' after a popular Japanese folk hero, a boy who battled demons. Flying the Ki-43 (as seen here), his score had risen to 33 by the time he returned to Japan in February 1944. Anabuki was to claim six more victories in the Ki-84 whilst ferrying them to the Philippines as a sergeant major flying instructor at Akeno. Post-war, he reached the rank of major in the JSDAF. In recent years the accuracy of Anabuki's claims has been challenged, and controversy surrounds some of them (*Satoshi Anabuki via Yasuho Izawa*)

Sgt Maj Noburo Mune, seen here standing by a captured Blenheim IV in Burma, was another 3rd Chutai, 50th Sentai pilot who claimed his first victory in the Philippines – a P-40 shot down over Bataan in January 1942. He also went on to serve over Burma, claiming 14 victories by the end of 1943, when he was sent back to Japan to serve as a flying instructor. Mune was killed in November 1944 in the Philippines, having returned to combat flying the Ki-84 with the 200th Sentai (*Yasuho Izawa*)

Up to this point in the aerial campaign in the Philippines the 24th Sentai had reported four aircraft lost or damaged and only one officer killed, whilst the 50th listed 12 aircraft lost or damaged, one officer killed, two officers missing, three other ranks killed and four personnel wounded.

Eight Ki-27s of the 50th Sentai's 3rd Chutai attacked four P-40s over Bataan Field on 19 January, the USAAC fighters attempting to provide air cover for four more Curtiss machines that were flying in from Del Monte, via Cebu. The Americans identified their opponents as 'Zeros'. The P-40 of 20th PS pilot 2Lt Lloyd Stinson was damaged in furious combat with a succession of Japanese fighters, receiving several hits including one in the fuselage fuel tank and another that disabled the guns in his right wing, but he got back safely. During this fight Lt Noburo Mune shot down the P-40 flown by 2Lt Marshall Anderson, who managed to bail out over Bagac but was then strafed and killed in his parachute by two of the Ki-27s. Lt Mune went on to claim a total of 14 victories with the 50th Sentai over Burma, before joining the 200th Sentai in October 1944. Ironically, he was killed whilst attempting to defend the Philippines from being retaken by American forces on 19 November 1944.

On 9 February 1942 six Ki-27s of 2Lt Kanamaru's section of the 50th Sentai's 3rd Chutai bounced a flight of four P-40s returning to Bataan following their escort of Capt Jesus Villamor of the Philippine Army Air Corps (PAAC), who had been tasked with photographing Japanese heavy artillery positions at Ternate from a Stearman biplane trainer. The American pilots turned into the Japanese formation and began firing as it passed over them, then commenced a left hand turn to come around. The exceptional mobility of the Ki-27s, described by the American pilots as resembling Boeing P-26 Peashooters, caught them by surprise, and they were quickly followed into their turns and set upon by the nimble Japanese fighters.

Two of the Ki-27s went after Villamor, who had dived away to escape and was about to land. Lt David L Obert tried to shoot one of the Ki-27s off the tail of another P-40, but his guns jammed and he himself then came under attack, forcing him to evade in a turning dive. 2Lt Earl R Stone Jr went after another Ki-27 but was not seen again. He had pursued the fighter flown by Sgt Toshisada Kurosawa into cloud covering Mt Mariveles. Evading within the overcast conditions, the Japanese pilot managed to turn the tables on his opponent, emerging on the tail of the searching P-40 and firing at it. Both aircraft were then seen to fly into the cloud once again, and Lt Stone was either shot down by Sgt Kurosawa or flew into the Cogon Tarak Ridge.

After the mission Sgt Kurosawa was also listed as missing, and it is now apparent that he too had crashed into the ridge, as his remains and the wreckage of his Ki-27 were found there in 2007. Cpl Anabuki recalled the missing Sgt Kurosawa;

'Sgt Kurosawa was a handsome, baby-faced young man. He had fair skin and his face looked pale after shaving. In the barracks [at Clark Field, Pampanga], he always slept in a cot next to mine. From that day on the cot was empty, and I missed him a lot. At night, out of character, I often thought of the severe and relentless war, and of the mortality of men fighting in the vast sky.'

The pair of Ki-27s that had gone after Villamor fired at the Stearman as it was attempting to land, hitting it in both wings as it taxied into a revetment. Villamor and his photographer, MSgt Juan Abanes, made a hasty exit from the biplane.

After diving away, Lt Obert had managed to get his guns firing again and climbed back up towards the fight. He made an attack on a solitary Ki-27 before his guns jammed again and he had to break away for the second time. 2Lt Ben Brown, who had been leading the P-40 flight, fired at a Ki-27 in a beam attack from the Japanese fighter's left quadrant and then engaged another head on after passing over his first opponent. He then fired at a third Ki-27 as it was turning away. When Brown tried to turn with his foe the P-40 stalled and dropped out of the fight. Finally, 2Lt John Posten's fighter was shot up and he had to land at San Jose.

Upon returning to their airfield, the pilots of 2Lt Kanamaru's section claimed that they had fought with nine P-40s, shooting down three of them. 2Lt Kanamaru claimed one and Cpl Anabuki was credited with two, but 2Lt Stone was the only American pilot actually lost. The sole Japanese fatality was Sgt Kurosawa, but 2Lt Kanamaru had to force land at Pilar as a result of damage sustained in the fight, and his Ki-27 was later destroyed by American artillery. WO Nakaue's fighter had also sustained damage, but he managed to return to Clark Field.

On 7 March the 50th Sentai's 3rd Chutai transferred its ten Ki-27s from Clark Field to Zablan to undertake air defence duties over Manila. The following month (2 April) the unit was attached to the 22nd Hikodan for final operations over Bataan, flying CAP sorties of five or six aircraft at most – other duties included the dropping of leaflets urging surrender. Less than a week later the Chutai handed over its remaining aircraft to six pilots from the 84th DHC who had arrived from Hanoi. Its personnel then rejoined the main force of the 50th Sentai, which by then was based at Mingaladon, in Burma.

Looking more like a row of sports aeroplanes from the 1930s than frontline fighters, a trio of Ki-27s from the 84th DHC are warmed up ready for flight by mechanics (*Summer*)

The 84th DHC was formed from within the 1st Chutai of the 64th Sentai in July 1939, which is why this Ki-27, photographed over China in the same year, carries the eagle motif of that unit. The 84th continued to use these markings when it was based in Hanoi from October 1940 until December 1942. From April to June 1942 it had sent pilots to serve in the Philippines flying ex-50th Sentai Ki-27s. The 84th began re-equipping with twin-engined Ki-45 fighters from January 1942, although it retained the Ki-27 on strength until at least June 1942, and possibly longer (*Hiroshi Sekiguchi via Yasuho Izawa*)

MALAYA, THE EAST INDIES AND BURMA

By December 1941 the JAAF had already begun to replace the Ki-27 with the more modern Nakajima Ki-43 Hayabusa (see *Aircraft of the Aces 85* for further details), but the obsolete-looking, fixed undercarriage fighter with its World War 1-era armament configuration still equipped 17 of the 19 fighter Sentai within the JAAF. Indeed, it formed the main fighter component of the JAAF during the air offensive against the British and Americans in Southeast Asia in 1941-42.

MALAYA AND SINGAPORE

The JAAF air component for the invasion of Malaya and Singapore and the drive down through the East Indies would be spearheaded by two units equipped with the new Ki-43, namely the 59th and 64th Sentais. The Hayabusa boasted an operational radius of 550-600 kilometres, its extended range being a strategic imperative for the JAAF. The need to replace the 'short-legged' Ki-27 had accelerated the development of the new fighter, which during the campaign would often be misidentified by Allied pilots as a Zero-sen.

The two Ki-27-equipped units that would add their strength to the campaign, the 1st and 11th Sentai of the 12th Hikodan (Air Brigade, but this unit is referred to as a 'Flying Battalion' or FB in some references) with 42 and 39 Ki-27 fighters, respectively, were more limited in range due to their fighters' operating radius of approximately 400 kilometres.

These range considerations had been played out in a map exercise held at the JAAF Staff College in January 1941 and presided over by Lt Col Kazuo Tanigawa, who had investigated the British air defence capability in Malaya in great detail during 1940. He would serve as a member of the air staff of the Southern General Army Headquarters during the offensive. In order to pursue the doctrine of 'aerial exterminating action' with the Ki-27, which represented 66 per cent of the fighter force available, it was essential that RAF airfields in Malaya be captured and secured at the earliest stages of the campaign.

'Aerial exterminating action' was envisaged as the 'positive and autonomous surveillance and complete destruction of enemy aircraft in the air and while still on the ground at their airfields'. It was intended to clear the way to permit air power to be used in a traditional ground support role without interference from enemy aircraft – what is now referred to in the JASDF of the 21st century as 'offensive counterair'. This doctrine was also largely responsible for the attacks on parachuting pilots that Allied aircrew found so repugnant, as the JAAF considered enemy aircrew to be a valuable asset to be eliminated at every opportunity, especially if parachuting to safety over their own territory.

Although the 'aerial exterminating action' doctrine had its origins in the *Annual Operation Plan* of 1935 and the *Air Troops Operations* guidance document of 1937, its adoption had been somewhat equivocated by the authorisation of *Air Operation Essentials* in 1940. This guidance manual, drawing on experience from Nomonhan, endorsed a balance between 'aerial exterminating action' and direct or close support of ground operations. Provision of the latter by the JAAF was to cause some tension between Army air and ground staff during the prosecution of air operations over Malaya.

Although the initial operational plan for the invasion of Malaya and Singapore had given priority to the ground support role, both Tanigawa and Lt Gen Michioho Sugawara (commander of the 3rd Air Division supporting the 15th and 25th Armies) worked to ensure that in practice the principles of 'aerial exterminating action' were followed. The air component was kept largely independent of direct ground forces control, operating almost as an 'air force' in its own right. The joint Army-Navy agreement for operations in Malaya set out that from the beginning of hostilities the 3rd Air Division would 'attack enemy aerodromes in northern Malaya, shoot down hostile aeroplanes and protect the landing of the Army's main forces'. Thenceforth, the main strength of the air division was to 'engage and secure domination over the enemy air force'.

Sgt Maj Iwataro Hazawa participated in the attack on Hong Kong with the 10th DHC, and continued to serve in the unit in China following its re-designation as the 25th Sentai, becoming one of its leading aces. As a warrant officer he had been credited with more than ten victories, plus up to 30 claims for damaging enemy aircraft. Hazawa had received a special citation from the 5th Air Army CO by the time he was killed in action at Hankow on 14 January 1945. He was attacked as he took off in response to a large-scale air raid by Fourteenth Air Force aircraft. Although he managed to bail out of his burning fighter, Hazawa's damaged parachute failed. He was posthumously promoted to second lieutenant (*Yasuho Izawa*)

In order to achieve both aims, the securing of airfields in southern Thailand, the Kra Isthmus and northern Malaya was seen as a priority objective for ground forces, and in furtherance of this JAAF 3rd Air Division ground personnel and equipment were included within the landing forces of the 5th Division at Singora. Their assignment to two troopships was not without its problems, however, as embarkation staff complained that they were loading 'even iron beds, bathtubs and sofas' onto the troopships!

In addition to bringing in support units with the leading waves, the JAAF negotiated for the allocation of an infantry battalion and a platoon of engineers from the 5th Division to assist in making the captured airfields ready for operations. Japanese flexibility in deploying their air power this way was not lost on the Allies. The C-in-C Far East, Air Chief Marshal Sir Robert Brooke-Popham, informed an early emergency conference that he 'had been amazed by the speed at which, according to intelligence reports, the Japanese air forces could both transfer aircraft from base to base and improvise new ones. People must remember that'.

The 12th Hikodan had moved onto airfields in western Indochina (now Vietnam) in preparation for the offensive. The 12-victory Nomonhan ace Goro Nishihara was now attached to the HQ of the 12th Hikodan, and he would fly as wingman to its commander, Col Buzo Aoki. Frustratingly for Nishihara, he would fail to engage the enemy in combat throughout the forthcoming campaign.

The 11th Sentai, commanded by Maj Tadashi Okabe, was at Cura Can airfield (sometimes called Kukan) on Phu Quoc Island, which was just off the Indochina coast on the eastern side of the Gulf of Siam (now Thailand). The 1st Sentai, commanded by Maj Kinshiro Takeda, was based at the mainland airfield of Tani Kep, inland from the coast near Kampong Trach (now in Cambodia).

These units were initially tasked with providing convoy escorts and CAPs for the 28 ships carrying the Japanese invasion forces across the Gulf of Siam. The Ki-27-equipped 77th Sentai was also committed to this important task, its 27 fighters being temporarily attached to the 12th Hikodan for this purpose. The 77th, commanded by Maj Yoshioka Hirose, was part of the 10th FB, which was scheduled to support the overland advance of the 15th Army through Thailand into Burma. In order to fulfil the preliminary convoy escort tasking it had been assigned, the 77th's 1st and 3rd Chutais, together with the Sentai HQ, moved to the airfield at Duong Dong, on Phu Quoc Island, leaving the 2nd Chutai behind at Sana, on Hainan Island.

On the morning of 7 December 1941, some 20 miles off Panjang Island (south of Phu Quoc), IJNAF Aichi E13A ('Jake') seaplane ZI-26, flown by Ens Eiichi Ogata, from the *Kamikawa Maru* engaged Catalina flying boat FY-V/W8417 of No 205 Sqn RAF. The latter, flown by Flg Off P E Bedell, had taken off from Seletar, in Singapore, in search of the Japanese invasion convoys. After the attack the Catalina flew away to the west, shadowed by Ogata, until a patrol of 1st Sentai Ki-27s spotted it.

Leading the five JAAF fighters was Lt Toshirou Kubotani, who was accompanied by WO Hirano, Sgt Maj Haruo Sato and Cpls Fujimoto and Yoshida. Sgt Maj Sato saw the Catalina first, and he was fired on by its gunners as he approached to look it over, causing him to veer away. Lt Kubotani then attacked the Catalina from above and astern, his rounds hitting the wing, which began to burn. Sgt Maj Sato returned to conduct a beam attack on the flying boat. Finally, WO Hirano led the trio of remaining Ki-27s in a stern attack, their combined weight of fire causing the Catalina to explode in flames and crash into the sea. There were no survivors from the crew of eight, and they had had no time to signal that they were under attack by Japanese aircraft. The Ki-27 had scored the first aerial victory of the Pacific War.

During the early morning hours of 8 December the Japanese Army's 5th and 18th Divisions began disembarking at landing beaches on the east coast of Thailand. Additionally, the Takumi Detachment consisting of the 56th Infantry Regiment and other elements of the 18th Division began landing at Khota Bharu, in northeastern Malaya, with the express purpose of capturing the airfield there. At about the same time a regiment of the 55th Division would land at four locations on the Kra Isthmus to seize three airfields there as a failsafe in case the landings further south were unsuccessful. The Imperial Guards Division of the 15th Army would cross the Thai border from Indochina (in present day Cambodia) and began advancing overland towards Bangkok.

Lt Masao Okumura and his Ki-27 Otsu of the 10th DHC immediately before the attack on Hong Kong. The unit retained its distinctive red-painted wheel fairings when some of the aircraft were camouflaged in dark green prior to the attack. Note the presentation legend *Aikoku (Patriotism) 396 (Tetsukuzu Tosei) 5001*, preserved by masking before the dark green camouflage was applied so that it appears on rectangles of the original grey-green paint (*Masao Oishi via Yasuho Izawa*)

Covering this advance, and now once again part of the 10th Hikodan, Maj Hirose led 11 Ki-27s from the 77th and 11th Sentais as escorts for nine Ki-30 light bombers of the 31st Sentai in a show of force from the Cambodian airfield at Siem Reap towards the Thai airfield at Aranyapraphet, with instructions to fight only if they encountered resistance. Three Curtiss Hawk III biplane fighters of the Royal Thai Air Force's 43rd Squadron, flown by Flt Lts Chai Soonthornsing and

Pilots of the 10th DHC relax in the sunshine at Canton after their successful attacks against Hong Kong. Sgt Maj Hazawa is seated in the front row, second from right. Lt Okumura is standing in the back row, second from the right, and next to him on the right is Sgt Kyushiro Ohtake. The latter served in the 10th DHC and 25th Sentai throughout the war in China, claiming at least ten victories. He was severely wounded in action over Seoul, Korea on 13 August 1945, and although he survived, Ohtake eventually succumbed to his injuries in 1951. The Chutai leader, Capt Yutaka Kozuki, is seated in the middle row, third from the left (*Masao Oishi via Yasuho Izawa*)

Chin Jiramanimai and PO Sanit Pothivaekoon, immediately took off against advice to engage the encroaching Japanese force. After a brief engagement the three Thai Hawks were shot down by Maj Hirose, 1Lt Yoshiro Kuwabara (the 3rd Chutai leader) and Lt Tsuguo Kojima, each claiming a victory. All three Thai pilots were killed.

This was 1Lt Kuwabara's first victory, the 24-year-old JAAF Academy graduate going on to become the 77th's most successful pilot in the aerial campaign over Burma, claiming a total of 12 victories by 26 February 1942. Later promoted to captain and given command of the 3rd Chutai of the 77th, flying the Ki-43, Kuwabara was to claim a P-38 probable and a P-47 destroyed in air combat over New Guinea. He also had the dubious distinction of being claimed as a probable or damaged by leading American ace Richard Bong during an encounter near But airfield on 5 March 1944, from which he narrowly escaped in his shot up Hayabusa by exhibiting exceptional flying skill. Kuwabara was to be reported missing in action, killed in combat with B-24s and P-47s over New Guinea, on 12 March 1944 whilst flying as executive officer of the 77th. During this combat the American pilots described their opponents from the 77th Sentai as 'experienced and very aggressive, the best encountered in combat so far' and that they had pushed home their attacks closely with 'brilliantly executed manoeuvres'.

Maj Hirose had claimed one of the first victories of the JAAF in a Ki-10 over Taiyuan, China, on 19 September 1937, for which his unit, the Miwa Daitai, had received many congratulatory telegrams. After leading the 77th in operations over Burma he was posted to command the 64th Sentai in March 1943 (see *Aircraft of the Aces 85* for further details). Following his return to Japan in June 1944 to serve as an instructor at the Akeno Flying School, Hirose was killed ramming a B-29 on 22 December 1944 (see *Aircraft of the Aces 100*). At the time of his death he had claimed a total of nine victories.

Following the Japanese landings in Thailand the airfield at Singora was quickly occupied, allowing the Ki-27s of the 1st and 11th Sentais to stage in whilst it was still coming under desultory Thai artillery fire. The tasking for the 12th Hikodan made its priorities clear;

'A. Enemy air power exterminating campaign.

'B. Gain air security in battlefield areas. Depending on the situation, concentrate on areas where troops are gathered.

'C. Participate in ground operation when necessary (this will be carried out only in favourable terrain).'

The two units were soon deployed on bomber escorts in Sentai strength and free-ranging fighter sweeps in Chutai and Shotai strength over enemy airfields in northern Malaya. The apparently haphazard nature of some of these combined sweep and airfield attack operations is belied by the systematic intelligence gathering and planning behind them. The rapid capture of British airfields in northern Malaya, aided in some cases by their premature evacuation and the abandonment of intact aviation fuel dumps and stores, was decisive in giving the shorter ranged Japanese aircraft a foothold when it came to operating over the battlefield and achieving air superiority.

The RAF fighter defence of Malaya and Singapore rested with four squadrons of Brewster Buffaloes, an American fighter originally designed for carrier operations (see *Aircraft of the Aces 91* for further details). The RAF had 126 Buffaloes available, of which only 79 were serviceable and ready for operations. These machines were divided between four squadrons and a maintenance unit. The frontline units were No 243 Sqn and No 488 Sqn Royal New Zealand Air Force (RNZAF) at Kallang, on Singapore island, with a detachment from the former unit at Khota Baru, No 453 Sqn Royal Australian Air Force (RAAF) at Sembawang, also on Singapore, and No 21 Sqn RAAF at Sungei Patani. This unit had only recently converted to the Buffalo from the two-seat Wirraway. These dispositions, and the ongoing need for fighter defence over Singapore, would seriously impede the RAF's ability to counter the Japanese 'aerial exterminating action' as it proceeded relentlessly southwards over Malaya.

Tactically, the Ki-27 units operated in flights (Shotai) of three aircraft, adopting a looser variation of the classic 'vic' formation. Each Shotai was usually led by an officer, who had an experienced NCO as his wingman and a novice or cadet pilot watching and learning in the third fighter. Many of the officers and NCOs had fought in air combat over China and Nomonhan and were supremely confident in their capability on type after three to five years of operational experience flying the Ki-27. Even so, the air fighting over Malaya was not the absolute walkover that has routinely been portrayed in the history books.

The much-maligned Buffalo was able to disengage by diving away at higher speeds and at steeper angles than the Ki-27, and compared to the Japanese fighter it had more powerful armament. The Japanese use of optical telescopic gunsights that pilots had to look through closely in order to aim reduced their situational awareness during combat, although this disadvantage was militated somewhat by the superior number of fighters that JAAF units were often able to deploy in battle against their Allied opponents.

On 8 December Ki-27s of the 11th Sentai claimed two Buffaloes 'turned back' over Sungei Patani – probably W8232 and W8212 of No 21 Sqn RAAF, flown by Flt Lt J R Kinninmont and Sgt N R Chapman, respectively (some sources refer to these aircraft being claimed as shot down). Both Buffaloes were shot up and damaged, but they were able to return to Sungei Patani. On 9 December Ki-27s from the 1st and 11th Sentais escorted two formations of Ki-21 bombers that attacked the RAF airfield at Butterworth.

In combat over the target with four Buffaloes of No 21 Sqn RAAF, Nomonhan veteran and 12-victory ace Sgt Maj Tokuyasu Ishizuka of the 11th Sentai's 3rd Chutai claimed two fighters shot down, although his own Ki-27 was damaged and he had to force land. His attacker was possibly Flg Off H V Montefiore, who claimed a Ki-27 but whose own aircraft (W8236) was hit shortly thereafter, forcing him to bail out. Once on the ground, Sgt Maj Ishizuka managed to evade Allied troops and return to his unit with the aid of local civilians. Sgt Maj Ishizuka was invalided back to Japan with sickness a short while later, but he subsequently recovered sufficiently to participate in the air defence of Japan as an instructor flying the Ki-45 Toryu. During these sorties from Hamamatsu he claimed a B-29 shot down, thus increasing his score to 15. Ishizuka survived the war, despite having been shot down no less than five times.

Flt Lt C R McKenny (W8224) was also shot down by Ki-27s on 8 December 1941 after attacking the bomber formation, although he managed to bail out. Flt Lt F H Williams' Buffalo (W8232) was strafed and burnt on the airfield by a shotai of three Ki-27s that followed him down after a dead stick landing with engine failure. Flt Lt Max White force landed on Penang Island in badly shot up Buffalo AN188, which was nevertheless categorised as repairable.

Naoharu Shiromoto, an 11-victory Nomonhan ace in the 1st Sentai, claimed a Buffalo shot down in the vicinity of Alor Star on 9 December. Either the location was incorrectly recorded or Shiromoto's claim relates to an incident on 12 December, when a lone Buffalo of No 4 Photo-Reconnaissance Unit, flown by Flt Lt Tony Phillips, was intercepted by a shotai of 1st Sentai Ki-27s near that location whilst on a reconnaissance sortie to Singora. Phillips identified his attackers as 'ME 110s', the spatted undercarriage of the Ki-27 perhaps giving him a fleeting impression of twin engines or twin fins. He was able to evade them after diving into cloud.

Shiromoto also claimed two Blenheims over Singora on 9 December in an engagement where the 1st Sentai was credited with downing five bombers from a mixed formation of six aircraft from Nos 34 and 60 Sqns (which had pooled their machines). Three Blenheim IVs were actually lost, No 60 Sqn's Sgt A McC Johnstone (V5931) force landing following an attack by Ki-27s and squadronmate Flt Lt J A B Dobson (V5589) being shot down (his crew perished but he was captured and reportedly beheaded by the Japanese). Sqn Ldr F O'Driscoll (V5829) of No 34 Sqn crash-landed his aircraft on its return flight as a result of damage received in combat.

Shiromoto would eventually claim 21 victories in total, including two P-38s shot down and two more that he caused to collide in a single-handed combat over Munda, New Guinea, on 31 January 1943. After service on Homeland Defence duties and with the 52nd Sentai, he ended the war with a Flying Training Unit in Korea. Following the Japanese surrender at war's end, Shiromoto was imprisoned by the Soviet authorities until 1947 for his part in the Nomonhan fighting.

Also flying with the 1st Sentai during the Malayan campaign was Nomonhan ace and Golden Kite award recipient Toshio Matsuura, who was now a sergeant major. He continued to make claims over Malaya and the East Indies, after which he participated in the Burma campaign and then flew Ki-43s over New Guinea. Returning to Japan in 1943 with claims of at least 15 victories, Matsuura was killed in an accident on 2 December that same year.

On 13 December 1941 a combined force of 1st and 11th Sentai Ki-27s conducted a sweep over Butterworth, but were bounced by Flt Lt T A 'Tim' Vigors and Sgt M D O'Mara. These two No 453 Sqn Buffaloes were part of a detachment of five that had been sent here from Sembawang under the leadership of Battle of Britan ace Vigors. Having only just landed at Butterworth, the Buffalo pilots quickly scrambled and scattered when warned of the incoming sweep. Vigors and O'Mara joined up, however, and were able to climb above and behind the Japanese formation, making their attack through scattered cloud.

Vigors thought he had hit several of the JAAF fighters as he dove through the formation to break it up, but he was quickly shot down by the Ki-27s. He managed to bail out of his blazing Buffalo, and although wounded and burnt, Vigors survived being strafed by the Japanese both as he descended by parachute and then once he was on the ground. O'Mara's Buffalo was also attacked and damaged in the fight, but he evaded and force landed at Kuala Kangsar.

Flt Lt B A Grace was attacked at low level by a Shotai from the 1st Sentai shortly after taking off, but he claimed to have shot down one of the Japanese fighters before his own aircraft was damaged and he had to evade. Lt Tomoichiro Fujisaki, 2nd Chutai leader of the 1st Sentai, was indeed killed during this engagement, apparently falling victim either to Vigors or Grace. Plt Off Geoff Angus was also caught flat-footed as he attempted to climb, enduring several attacking passes by a Shotai of Ki-27s before pancaking into a paddy field. Here, his aircraft was strafed by a single fighter. Sgt Ron Oelrich was attacked in the same way, but in attempting to lead his attackers over the airfield's anti-aircraft defences he was himself shot down and killed by the Bofors guns.

By 2 January the Japanese had occupied Kuantan, on the east coast of Malaya, and the 1st and 11th Sentais moved in from Singora soon afterwards to occupy it as their main base for the rest of the campaign.

On the morning of 12 January both units put up a combined total of 72 Ki-27s for a sweep over Singapore, and the 11th Sentai caught a formation of eight Buffaloes of No 488 Sqn climbing to intercept them. The Ki-27 pilots claimed ten Buffaloes in this engagement, when in fact two had been shot down and five damaged. The details of the claimants are unknown, although Naoharu Shiromoto of the 1st Sentai's 3rd Chutai claimed a victory over Singapore during January to raise his score to 15. Both of the pilots that were shot down, Sgt T Honan in W8200 and Sgt R MacMillan in W8186, managed to bail out successfully. Plt Off H S Pettit found he could evade the Ki-27s by diving away, but on each of the three occasions he attempted to climb in order to attack again he was bounced and forced to evade, eventually being wounded. This no doubt contributed to the Japanese claims.

Another sweep was made in the afternoon, and this time the Ki-27s clashed with RAF Buffaloes of No 243 Sqn and three Dutch Brewster 339s (the export version of the Buffalo) of 2-VIG-V. The Dutch pilots claimed four Ki-27s destroyed, but Lt A Deibel was in turn shot down – although wounded, he managed to bail out. The RAF pilots claimed two destroyed and one probable for the loss of Sgt N Rankin in W8189/Q, who was killed. Buffalo W8187/R, flown by Sgt M J F Baldwin, was damaged.

On another fighter sweep on 15 January Ki-27 pilots of the 1st Sentai claimed seven Buffaloes destroyed from a flight of 13 engaged over Singapore. The aircraft were either from No 488 Sqn or No 243 Sqn, both of which reported engagements with Ki-27s. Neither unit lost any aircraft, and their pilots in turn claimed two Ki-27s destroyed, although the JAAF suffered no losses.

From 26 January the 12th Hikodan provided rotational CAP over a landing force at Endau that was bringing in the 96th Airfield Battalion and quantities of equipment and stores intended to make the airfields at Kahang and Kluang serviceable once they were captured.

The RAF mounted a series of four desperate raids against the ships of this landing force, using all the bombers it had available. The first raid, and its escorting fighters, was met by nine Ki-27s of the 11th Sentai's 2nd Chutai, led by Capt Michiaki Tojo, and ten Ki-27s of the 1st Sentai's 2nd Chutai under Capt Takejiro Koyanagi. The latter, who was the Sentai's executive officer, was also temporarily commanding the Chutai so as to mentor Capt Tatsuti Yamashita, who had only recently taken command after the previous Chutai leader's loss on 13 December. Before becoming executive officer, Koyanagi had led the 2nd Chutai from August 1939 to May 1941.

The Japanese flyers claimed two Hudsons, two Vildebeest, five Buffaloes and two Hurricanes shot down, and three more Vildebeest forced to crash-land. WO Hitoshi Tobita of the 11th Sentai's 2nd Chutai, who had scored seven victories over Nomonhan, claimed one of the Vildebeest shot down during this raid. It was his last claim, as following a bout of illness he became a flying instructor. A second Vildebeest raid later in the day was opposed by ten Ki-27s of the 1st Sentai's 3rd Chutai. During this combat Naoharu Shiromoto claimed two kills to bring his score to 17. Lt Mizotani of the 1st Sentai was forced to bail out and 1Lt Toshiro Kuboya was severely wounded. The latter pilot managed to return to base but succumbed to his injuries three weeks later. Three other Ki-27s were also damaged by return fire.

During the afternoon of 28 January 22-victory Nomonhan ace Sgt Maj Zenzaburo Ohtsuka of the 11th Sentai was killed during a raid on Kuantan by four B-17s from the 7th and 19th BGs, the bombers having flown from Malang, via Palembang. 1Lts Kikuo Koga, Hiroshi Ono and Cpl Hatsushi Haraguchi were also killed during the raid, with an additional 27 personnel being wounded. The bombs fell amongst the Ki-27s as they were attempting to take off to intercept the bombers, destroying one aircraft and damaging nine, three of them seriously.

The Ki-27s of the 12th Hikodan continued to operate over Malaya from Kuantan and Kuala Lumpur until the RAF evacuation of Singapore. On 6 February the 1st Sentai's 1st Chutai engaged two Hurricanes from No 232 Sqn near Kallang, claiming one shot down. The aircraft flown by Sgt I D Newlands was indeed damaged, but the pilot managed to land safely, whilst Plt Off M C Fitzherbert in the second Hurricane claimed a Ki-27 destroyed. No 232 Sqn conducted a second patrol over Kallang later in the day, and it too was engaged by Ki-27s, although they were identified as Zero-sens – Sgt F Margarson claimed one as damaged. The Ki-27 pilots claimed another Hurricane as a probable, but 1st Chutai leader Capt Goro Okazawa and 1Lt Tadao Tomizawa failed to return, possibly having fallen victim to Fitzherbert and Margarson.

After the fall of Singapore on 15 February 1942, elements of the 12th Hikodan moved down into the East Indies to support operations there. The bulk of the air fighting in the theatre, however, fell to the Zero-sens of the IJNAF and the Ki-43 'Oscars' of the 59th and 64th Sentais, with the Ki-27s being mainly tasked with providing CAP over airfields, convoys and troop landing areas.

On 15 February eight Ki-27s flying from Palembang P1 airfield and patrolling over the Banka Island landings claimed two 'Buffaloes' shot down out of four engaged. The Japanese detachment included recently promoted ten-victory Nomonhan ace 1Lt Yutaka Aoyagi, who was now leading a Shotai. The 'Buffaloes' were in fact Hurricanes from No 232 Sqn, and the RAF pilots in turn claimed two Ki-27s destroyed. However, all the Japanese aircraft returned to Palembang P1, although two machines that had been damaged in the fight crash-landed there. Lt Aoyagi also claimed a Blenheim IV destroyed that same day, possibly from a formation of three No 211 Sqn aircraft engaged over Palembang – none were actually lost.

The following day four Martin Model 139 bombers (a Dutch version of the USAAC's B-10) from 3-VlG-III (*Vliegtuiggroep* (VLG) – Aircraft Group) flew a mission to attack the airfield at Palembang P1 and shipping off the Moesi estuary. As they neared the target they were attacked by Ki-27s from the airfield, and Lt Aoyagi, leading one of the elements, claimed a 'Hudson'. This might have been Model 139 M-578, flown by Sgt J Bakker, which failed to return.

On 17 February eight Ki-27s of the 11th Sentai encountered eight bomb-carrying P-40s of the 17th PS (Provisional), led by Maj C A Sprague, which were attacking shipping in the Moesi Delta. Sprague, Capts G McCallum and W L Coss and Lt J Kruzel dropped their tanks and bombs as ordered upon sighting the Ki-27s, but Capt G Mahony and Lts H J Egenes, G E Kiser and W J Hennon dropped their tanks only, retaining their bombs. The resulting combat lasted barely three minutes, during which time the American pilots found it difficult to line up on the Ki-27s, only six of which had engaged. Coss described how, when he fired at the Ki-27, the fighter 'would pull up and climb at an angle I could not follow'.

Four of the P-40 pilots, including Sprague, claimed victories and one claimed two probables, but only a single Ki-27 was lost, with the pilot successfully bailing out. This was possibly the fighter that Hennon had 'hit very hard' at low level near Palembang P1 after dropping out of the dogfight, this Ki-27 being one of a pair of JAAF fighters that had hung back from the initial combat. The Japanese pilots claimed three P-40s shot down, but none were lost, only one aircraft suffering four 7.7 mm hits to its upper fuselage. After this encounter, and despite the Ki-27's manoeuvrability, the P-40 pilots felt that their fighters completely outclassed the 'Type 97s'.

The following day the remainder of the 11th Sentai (16 Ki-27s) flew in to Palembang P1, and within two days the unit had moved to Tandjoekarang (now Bandar Lamang).

A mixed formation of seven RAF Blenheim IVs from Nos 34, 84 and 211 Sqns was intercepted over Palembang P1 on 19 February by Ki-27s, the bomber gunners claiming four fighters shot down, although the JAAF reported no pilot fatalities. All the bombers returned from the mission, but the No 34 Sqn aircraft flown by Flt Lt M K Holland was badly damaged. That same day Ki-27s intercepted three Dutch Martin Model 139s targeting Pladjoe refinery. M-533 of 3-VlG-III, flown by Tlt vl wnr (Tweede Luitenant Vlieger Waarnemer – Second Lieutenant Pilot Observer) P J P van Erkel was attacked after a successful bombing run, but the aircraft managed to escape undamaged into cloud. M-568, flown by L Davids, was attacked in the same incident, and although damaged the bomber also managed to get away.

Lt Aoyagi claimed a Blenheim IV shot down over Palembang P1 on 24 February, the aircraft being one of three No 84 Sqn bombers targeting the airfield. Flown by Flg Off B Fihelly, the Blenheim IV was attacked by Aoyagi's shotai of three Ki-27s as it was making its bombing run. The JAAF pilots exchanged fire with the gunner, Sgt E Oliver (who believed he had also scored a probable), hitting the bomber's starboard engine before it managed to escape into cloud. The damaged engine was streaming oil, however, and when the propeller came off Fihelly had to ditch the Blenheim in the sea. Another Shotai of Ki-27s attacked the Blenheim flown by Sqn Ldr A K Passmore over the target but he was able to get away.

The next day Aoyagi claimed a 'Hudson' when his CAP of six Ki-27s attacked four Dutch Martin Model 139s attacking Pladjoe refinery, Ens Th Magnee of 2-VlG-III being shot down. On the 27th Martin Model 139 M-524 of 3-VlG-III was attacked and damaged by three Ki-27s over Palembang P1, the pilot, Lt P J P van Erkel, successfully belly landing the aircraft with a full bomb load on board. One of the Ki-27s was damaged by return fire from the bomber.

On 28 February six patrolling Ki-27s caught Dutch Catalina Y-63 of GVT-2 at low level returning from a reconnaissance mission over Banka Island and the Banka Strait, and in a running fight forced it down on the water, where it sank. The Catalina crew claimed a Ki-27 shot down and another damaged during this fight, but there were no reported Japanese fatalities.

By 10 March the 12th Hikodan had starting transferring to Burma to reinforce the JAAF's aerial campaign there. Lt Aoyagi survived the Malayan and East Indies campaigns, adding more victories to his Nomonhan total. In April 1942 he transferred to the newly formed Kyodo (Training) 204th Sentai at Zhenxi, in Manchuria, and on 23 June that same year he was accidentally shot down and killed by another Ki-27 pilot whilst towing a drogue target during a gunnery training exercise.

BURMA

After their preliminary operations over Thailand, the 77th Sentai concentrated at Don Muang airfield on the outskirts of Bangkok as it prepared to support the invasion of Burma. On 11 December 1941 the whole Sentai flew an offensive sweep over the Burmese city of Tavoy (now Dawei) and strafed aircraft at a nearby airfield, destroying a North American Yale trainer of the Burma Volunteer Air Force. Anti-aircraft fire damaged four of the Ki-27s and mortally wounded WO Kikuji Kishida, who died shortly after returning to Don Muang.

For operations against Rangoon and south-central Burma, the 77th moved to the northwest and central Thai airfields of Tak (Raheng) and

77th Sentai pilots relax on their airfield in Burma, perhaps after the recent air fighting had subsided. The mixture of uniform and civilian clothing is typical, such combinations being almost universal amongst service pilots of the JAAF during this era. The original print of this photograph reveals that two of the aircraft in the background have camouflaged wings and tailplanes (*Yasuho Izawa*)

Phitsanulok and, subsequently, to Lampang in the north, but retained a detachment at Don Muang. The fighter defence of Burma at this time was limited to the 16 Buffaloes of No 67 Sqn RAF and the 21 Curtiss Hawk 81-A-2 fighters of the Third Squadron, American Volunteer Group (AVG) – the famous 'Flying Tigers'.

On 23 December a major Japanese air raid was mounted against the airfield at Mingaladon, near Rangoon. No fewer than 60 Ki-21 'Sallys' from the 60th, 62nd and 98th Sentais and 27 Ki-30 'Annes' from the 31st Sentai took part in the mission, escorted by 30 Ki-27s from the 77th Sentai. To counter the raid 15 Buffaloes of No 67 Sqn and ten AVG Hawk 81-A-2s were scrambled. Managing to gain height before the attackers arrived, they initially intercepted the unescorted heavy bombers of the 62nd Sentai. Thereafter, the British and American pilots made sporadic passes at the Ki-30s at lower altitude, which were frequently misidentified as fighters, whilst the Ki-27s attempted to defend both the Ki-21s and their light bomber charges over the target area.

Sgt Vic Bargh, in No 67 Sqn Buffalo AN168 (not W8143 as reported elsewhere), was shot up by a Ki-27 from a group that closed on him after he had initially attempted to attack the bombers. He later recalled his first clash with the Ki-27;

'When I met the Japanese fighters, I was the only one [of the No 67 Sqn pilots] there, surrounded by about 30 enemy aircraft. The first ones that came in, we found out later, were called "Nates". They had fixed undercarriages – that's why they got onto me quick. They could just follow me around, a few feet behind. I couldn't handle them. They beat me, as I never fired my guns. There was a joker sitting behind me, but the harmonisation of his guns with his gunsight was so far down – they harmonised them at 250 yards or something like that – that the bullets just stripped the bottom of the aeroplane and never hit me. This was just as well as I never had any armour plating. It's hard to believe. Anyway, a bullet ricocheted up by my ear and hit the canopy, and I did a smart dive and left them behind.

'They had two guns firing through the bottom of the engine, and the joker had an Aldis sight that I could see – they were not very far away, and he was aiming at my tail. I don't reckon he was a top pilot – he was probably with a first-class lot of pilots, but he wouldn't have been as good as the leader, otherwise he'd have lifted his aim up a bit and I would have got the lot. So I got away with it.'

Bargh identified the fixed undercarriage aircraft he had encountered as 'Navy Type 96 fighters' in his logbook. Despite the damage to his Buffalo he was able to evade, wipe the oil from his windscreen with his sock, regain height and make further attacks against the Ki-21 formation, claiming one shot down. Bargh is also credited with a Ki-27 probable by one source, but he refutes this, stating that he did not even fire at the fighters, let alone hit one.

The AVG also identified the Japanese aircraft as 'Navy Type 96 fighters'. After attacking the bombers, the Hawk 81-A-2 pilots were in turn bounced by the Ki-27s, resulting in the death of Henry J Gilbert. Paul Greene claimed one of the Japanese fighters shot down and a second as a probable before his own aircraft was shot up by a third Ki-27 and he was forced to bail out. Several Buffaloes and Hawk 81-A-2s returned with damage either from the return fire of the bombers or from attacks by the Ki-27s.

During this confused fighting Maj Hirose claimed two kills and Capt Kaoru Kakimi, a pilot in the Hombu Shotai (HQ flight), was credited with another. Single kills were also claimed by 2nd Chutai leader Capt Mitsuhiro Matsuda, Lt Kuwabara for his second victory, Lts Shinjirou Nagoshi and Shigeru Suzuki and WOs Saburo Hagiwara and Honma, for a total of nine claims – seven 'Spitfires' and two Buffaloes, together with four probables and a fighter strafed on the ground. The Allied pilots were credited with one Japanese fighter shot down and two probables, but all the Ki-27s returned safely.

Although the presence of the AVG was known to Japanese intelligence, the pilots of the 77th were unaware that their opposition might include Hawk 81-A-2s, which they identified in their combat reports as 'Supittofaia' – Spitfires. In the aerial fighting over Burma, most JAAF pilots came to consider the AVG their strongest opponents, noting their aggression. They were also impressed with the diving speed of the Hawk 81-A-2s when compared to the RAF Buffalo and, later, Hurricane I/II. Despite this disadvantage, the Ki-27, with its twin rifle-calibre machine gun armament, had done rather well in this first encounter with the faster and more heavily armed enemy aircraft.

Two days later, on 25 December, the Japanese launched another large-scale raid against Rangoon. One formation consisted of 63 Ki-21s from the 12th and 60th Sentais, escorted by 25 Ki-43s from the 64th Sentai, with a second formation made up of eight Ki-21s from the 62nd Sentai and 27 Ki-30 light bombers from the 31st Sentai, escorted by 32 Ki-27s from the 77th Sentai.

Pilots from the latter Sentai claimed seven Allied fighters destroyed and four probables from those encountered in the ensuing dogfights, which occurred at multiple altitudes and involved

Toyoki Eto became leader of the 1st Chutai, 77th Sentai in June 1940, having previously claimed two victories over China whilst flying the Ki-10 (examples of which can be seen here behind Eto). The unit converted to the Ki-27 in Manchuria in late 1939, and Capt Eto flew the type throughout the invasion of Burma, claiming six aircraft shot down and five probables – some of these were shared with other pilots. After serving at Akeno as an instructor Eto was promoted to major, and in June 1944 he took command of the 64th Sentai. Eto survived the war (*Yasuho Izawa*)

Pilots of the 77th Sentai parade in front of their camouflaged Ki-27s during operations over Burma in early 1942. Note the Toyota KC starter trucks. The Japanese had made provision for JAAF ground service personnel, vehicles and equipment to be landed early with the invasion forces in Malaya in order to quickly exploit captured airfields. The speed and flexibility with which they accomplished this was noted with astonishment by staff officers of the British Army (*Yasuho Izawa*)

both JAAF fighter units. Lt Kisaji Beppu was credited with one victory, as were Lts Yoshihide Matsuo and Tsuguo Kojima, Sgt Majs Matsunaga and Akamatsu (who also claimed a probable) and Sgts Niino and Ono. Probables were also claimed by 1st Chutai leader Capt Toyoki Eto, 2nd Chutai leader Capt Mitsuhiro Matsuda and WO Kitasaka. The 77th lost two pilots – Lt Masashi Someya, who was killed in action, and Sgt Maj Kontetu Ri who bailed out and was captured. Sgt Ono's Ki-27 was also badly damaged, and he had to force land upon returning to Thailand. In total, the RAF had four Buffaloes destroyed and two badly damaged and the AVG lost two Hawk 81-A-2s and had four more damaged, against claims for 12 Japanese fighters shot down.

Capt Eto had scored his first two kills with the 77th over China on 21 August 1938 whilst flying the Ki-10, shooting down two Chinese-flown I-16s over Hankow. He had no further opportunities for air combat, and following conversion to the Ki-27 at the end of 1939 Eto attended a commanders' course at Akeno and was promoted to lead the 1st Chutai. Following the first Burma campaign, during which he was to claim 11 victories (including probables and shared kills), he would return to Akeno as a flying instructor. In June 1944 Eto was posted back to Burma as a major to take command of the famous 64th Sentai, then flying the Ki-43, and on 9 January 1945 he claimed a Spitfire of No 67 Sqn for a total of 12 victories. He returned to Japan in April 1945 and survived the war.

On 2 January 1942 nine Ki-27s of the 1st Chutai of the 77th, under Capt Eto's leadership, moved from Lampang to the forward airfield at Raheng (Tak). The following day the fighters attacked Moulmein airfield, strafing six biplanes they spotted on the ground. Lt Kisaji Beppu claimed to have set one alight, and the remaining five were damaged by the other Chutai pilots. No 4 Coastal Defence Flight of the Indian Air Force, occupying the airfield, reported that two Hawker Audaxes and two Westland Wapitis were destroyed in the attack.

As the Ki-27s were landing upon their return to Raheng, three AVG Hawk 81-A-2s arrived and began strafing the airfield. Lt Beppu's Shotai was preparing to land at the time, and one of its Ki-27s was badly hit by the AVG Second Squadron commander, Jack Newkirk, who claimed that it crashed into the trees beside the airfield. Newkirk then went after Lt Beppu, who looped and made a head-on run at the Hawk 81-A-2, claiming it as a probable. Sgt Maj Matsunaga attacked future ace Jim Howard's strafing Tomahawk and believed he had shot it down before he was driven off by the third Tomahawk flown by another future ace, 'Tex' Hill, who claimed the Ki-27 as destroyed.

Matsunaga had damaged the engine in Howard's Hawk 81-A-2, making it lose power to the point where he thought he would have to force land. But at low level the engine picked up and Howard was able to get away, returning with 7.7 mm hits to his engine, fuselage, tail and armour plating. No fatalities were reported by the JAAF, but on the ground one

Ki-27 had been destroyed, another badly damaged and a third slightly holed in the strafing attack.

Maj Hirose led the whole Sentai – 31 Ki-27s – on a retaliatory sweep over Rangoon on 4 January. As the Hombu Shotai and 3rd Chutai dropped down to strafe ground targets, they caught a flight of six AVG Hawk 81-A-2s climbing up below the clouds. Three American fighters were quickly shot down for no loss, the JAAF pilots claiming four and one probable – again, they identified the Hawk 81-A-2s as 'Spitfires'. WO Masao Hadeshima of the 3rd Chutai, flying on this occasion with the Hombu Shotai, claimed one, as did WOs Yoshida and Honma and Sgt Kobayakawa. Lt Shigeru Suzuki was credited with the probable.

George Paxton was wounded by a 7.7 mm round that split the seam in his armour plating, but he managed to dive away and force land his burning Hawk 81-A-2 on the field at Mingaladon, where it was subsequently written off. Bert Christman's fighter was riddled, knocking out its engine. As the Hawk 81-A-2's engine began to burn he bailed out, landing safely. Gil Bright's machine was also shot up, and he had to crash-land the burning fighter in a dried-up paddy field, escaping with a scorched face. The three remaining AVG pilots claimed hits on the Ki-27s before diving away, Ken Merritt receiving credit for shooting down George Paxton's attacker.

WO Masao Hadeshima of the 77th had already shared a claim with Lt Kiyoshi Nishikawa for a Soviet-flown Chinese SB bomber on 14 March 1938 whilst flying a Ki-10 with the 8th Daitai. Eight days after downing his Hawk 81-A-2, Hadeshima destroyed Catalina I W8409/Q of No 205 Sqn, flown by Sqn Ldr M F C Farrar DFC. He intercepted this machine during an evening patrol from Singora, having been detached there to perform air defence duties. Hadeshima would claim another P-40 probable on 21 February (see below), but he had still to reach ace status when he was killed in combat with P-51 Mustangs over Laohekou, China, on 4 January 1945 whilst flying with the 25th Sentai.

Although the 77th was operating successfully in the air, it suffered further losses (five Ki-27s destroyed and several more damaged) from AVG strafing attacks on 7 and 8 January. As a result of these raids, the 77th hastily began to camouflage its light grey-green aircraft in dark green and brown paints. On 7 January, following their participation in the Philippines campaign (see Chapter 3), the 1st and 2nd Chutais of the Ki-27-equipped 50th Sentai moved to Nakhorn Sawan, in Thailand, using Moulmein as a forward staging field to reinforce the JAAF fighter strength for the aerial campaign over Burma.

Seven Ki-27s from the 77th Sentai escorted Ki-30s from the 31st Sentai in a raid on the airfield at Tavoy on 19 January, the fighter unit having previously claimed seven aircraft destroyed on the ground when it strafed the base on the 13th. On the 19th the Japanese formation ran into a flight of six Blenheim IVs, escorted by two Buffaloes and a Hawk 81-A-2, which had been sent to Tavoy to evacuate ground staff but had become

After shooting down a Thai Curtiss Hawk III on 8 December 1941, 1Lt Yoshiro Kuwabara went on to become the 77th Sentai's most successful Ki-27 pilot during the invasion of Burma by claiming 12 aircraft downed by the end of February 1942, when the unit was withdrawn from operations. Kuwabara was lost in combat with B-24s and P-47s over Wewak, New Guinea, on 12 March 1944, by which time he was serving as the unit's executive officer with the rank of captain. His final score was in excess of 13 victories, including at least one P-47 Thunderbolt destroyed (*Yasuho Izawa*)

scattered in the murky haze. The Blenheim IVs all managed to dive away and evade, although Sqn Ldr Duggan Smith's aircraft was shot up as the Allied fighters engaged the Ki-27s in an inconsequential fight. A second AVG Hawk 81-A-2 flown by future ace Dick Rossi entered the dogfight in its final stages.

Capt Karao Kakimi of the Hombu Shotai claimed two enemy fighters shot down, whilst Sgt Maj Shibata of the 2nd Chutai claimed one. One Buffalo pilot had landed at Moulmein with a ruptured oil line. He was joined a short while later by Rossi, who helped him patch the Brewster up, before both men flew back to Mingaladon together.

The next day the 77th's 3rd Chutai hit Moulmein in a strafing attack, the Ki-27 pilots shooting down two No 67 Sqn Buffaloes that were attempting to take off after refuelling on the way back from a reconnaissance sortie over Raheng. Plt Off Paul Brewer, in W8229, was caught low and slow over the airfield, and Sgt John Finn, in W8240, who had cleared the airfield, bravely turned back to help him. Both pilots were killed.

Following this attack, the returning 3rd Chutai encountered a force of six Blenheim IVs from No 113 Sqn near Kawkereik on their way to bomb the Japanese airfield at Mesoht. They were escorted by six AVG Hawk 81-A-2s, whose pilots claimed three 'I-97s' destroyed and two probables. Robert Moss was subsequently forced to bail out of his Curtiss fighter on the return trip home, and a second Hawk 81-A-2 suffered serious battle damage. The optimistic Ki-27 pilots claimed four destroyed and one probable, with two of these victories being credited to the Sentai's most successful flyer, Lt Yoshiro Kuwabara, and one each to Lts Shigeru Suzuki and Shimoda, with the probable credited to Lt Jun-ichi Ogata. Moments after his credited victory, Lt Suzuki was shot down and killed.

Future ace Bob Neale, who was flying one of the Hawk 81-A-2s on this date, recalled that the Ki-27s were 'much slower than us, and it was easy to get away from them, but you couldn't turn with them. You could [only] make a pass at them and try to get them in your sights long enough to really hit them'.

On the morning of 23 January 24 Ki-27s from the 50th Sentai conducted a fighter sweep over the airfields at Rangoon, meeting Buffaloes, Hawk 81-A-2s and three newly arrived Hurricanes of No 17 Sqn RAF with their ferry tanks still attached. The Japanese claimed two 'P-40s' destroyed and one probable, plus one Buffalo and one 'Spitfire' destroyed, a second 'Spitfire' as a probable and an unidentified fighter destroyed. Allied losses were one Buffalo (W8239) shot down, killing ace Flt Lt D J C Pinckney, and one Hurricane badly damaged. The 50th lost two Ki-27s, with their pilots, Lt Minoru Niino and Sgt Maj Sadao Kimizuka, being killed.

Towards midday the 77th Sentai conducted its own sweep, which resulted in 24 Ki-27s engaging AVG Hawk 81-A-2s of the First and Second Squadrons, plus three No 67 Sqn Buffaloes, over Mingaladon. The 77th had in fact been tasked with escorting 12 Ki-30s of the 31st Sentai, but it had missed the rendezvous. Indeed, the Ki-27 pilots only caught up with the light bombers after they had already come under attack over Mingaladon.

The 77th claimed eight P-40s destroyed and four more as probables, although the AVG actually lost only three fighters in combat. Ace Jack

Newkirk crashed his shot up Hawk 81-A-2 when he tried to land, Bert Christman bailed out but was apparently killed in his parachute and ace Bill Bartling crash-landed his damaged aircraft. Noel Bacon's Hawk 81-A-2 was damaged, but he managed to return to base with 12 hits in his engine, cockpit and wings. 1st Chutai leader Capt Eto claimed three destroyed, Lt Beppu one destroyed and WO Kimura one probable, whilst the 2nd Chutai's Lt Yamamoto and WO Hagiwara were each credited with one destroyed and one probable. The 3rd Chutai's WO Honma and Sgt Maj Nagashima also claimed one destroyed each. The AVG pilots were credited with five destroyed and four probables, although not a single Ki-27 had in fact been lost. Following this action, pilots from the 77th concluded that their enemy 'had a great will to fight, but their technique in the air was not superior'.

A Ki-27 of the 1st Chutai, 50th Sentai at Moulmein, Burma, during January 1942. When the aircraft of this Chutai were camouflaged with dark green paint the unit's lightning bolt motif was masked off, leaving a narrow border of the original grey-green finish (*Mohei Takada via Yasuho Izawa*)

The pattern of action against the airfields around Rangoon was consistent and relentless, with the 'aerial exterminating action' consisting of escorted daylight heavy bomber raids at high altitude and light bomber raids at lower altitude, alternated with fighter sweeps and night bomber raids. So far pilots from the 77th had fared well in their Ki-27s, inflicting more losses than they had sustained in aerial combat – a remarkable achievement given their lightly armed aircraft. A number of nascent aces had emerged, including Eto, Kuwabara and Beppu. Even so, the Japanese acknowledged that the Allied fighters 'were superior to our Type 97s in speed, and for this reason we occasionally had difficulty in carrying out our air operations'.

Twenty-one Ki-27s from the 50th Sentai staged from Nakhon Sawon to Raheng to escort a small force of six Ki-21s raiding Rangoon on 24 January. The CO of the 50th Sentai, Maj Yasuho Makino, was badly injured when his Ki-27 lost power and crashed on takeoff from Raheng, so command of the escort devolved to the 1st Chutai leader, Capt Fujio Sakaguchi. The Ki-21s inexplicably beat their Ki-27 escorts to the target, where they were met by three AVG Hawk 81-A-2s, four Buffaloes and two Hurricanes. The unprotected JAAF bombers were devastated by the Allied fighters, which shot down five Ki-21s, including the aircraft flown by the formation leader. AVG aces 'Tex' Hill and Ed Rector tangled with the fighter escorts after hitting the bombers, each pilot emerging from the engagement with claims for a Ki-21 and a Ki-27 destroyed apiece. Three more Hawk 81-A-2 pilots went straight for the fighters, and claimed three destroyed for a total of five.

The 50th Sentai was indeed badly hurt by the AVG, losing three pilots (including Sakaguchi) for no claims, although two fighters scored hits on Bob Neale's Hawk 81-A-2, shooting the microphone away from his helmet.

Shortly thereafter a trio of Ki-30s escorted by 25 Ki-27s from the 77th Sentai arrived over Mingaladon and began strafing the field just as the Hurricanes flown by No 17 Sqn's CO, and ace, Sqn Ldr C A C 'Bunny' Stone DFC, and Plt Off D E Fuge were coming in to land. Eto claimed one of these destroyed, stating that his victim was a 'P-40', while WO Fujinaga was credited with the second RAF fighter as a probable. Both men got down safely, however, being unaware that they had even been attacked! Stone had earlier tangled with the 50th Sentai and had returned to base out of ammunition, having fought a fruitless duel with a Ki-27 and then briefly flown alongside it as it headed home also out of ammunition, making rude gestures, which were reciprocated by the Japanese pilot.

The final claim of the day was made by 77th Sentai pilot Lt Shinjirou Nagoshi, who destroyed a large aircraft on the ground at Mingaladon during one of his strafing runs.

The 50th Sentai sent 23 Ki-27s for a more effective sweep of Mingaladon on 26 January, the fighters bouncing four scrambled AVG Hawk 81-A-2s and three Hurricanes (still with their ferry tanks attached) as they were climbing. Two more AVG fighters that had separated from the main formation managed to climb above the Ki-27s and dive on them. The JAAF pilots claimed four aircraft shot down and six probables, although the AVG only lost two, with Bob Moss bailing out and Louis Hoffman being killed. The Hurricane flown by Sqn Ldr Stone was also badly shot up, but he managed to get down safely. The No 17 Sqn CO later recalled, 'I could not even manage to get my sights on them, and boy could they shoot'. Sgt Maj Kimiyoshi Araya of the 50th Sentai did not return, having probably been shot down by either Gil Bright, Bob Neale or Bill McGarry, as all three of these AVG aces claimed a fighter destroyed.

On 28 January the 77th Sentai again targeted Mingaladon, this time with 27 Ki-27s, whilst the 50th sent only ten. At 17,000 ft the Japanese fighters were confronted by no fewer than 16 Hawk 81-A-2s from two AVG squadrons and a pair of Hurricanes. The subsequent fighting took place within a 40-mile radius of Mingaladon.

Capt Eto claimed a probable and Lt Kuwabara another one confirmed, whilst Lts Beppu, Nakao and Matsuo and WO Hagiwara were also credited with one victory each for a total of seven kills and one probable, but the 77th lost 2nd Chutai leader Capt Mitsuhiro Matsuda, Lt Kanekichi Yamamoto and WO Takeshi Kitazaka. Seeing his Chutai leader under attack by three Hawk 81-A-2s, Lt Yamamoto had gone to his aid, but he was too late to prevent Matsuda from being shot down. The engine of Yamamoto's Ki-27 was then hit, and when it caught fire he deliberately dived into a Hawk 81-A-2 parked on the airfield in a jibaku (suicide crash drive). The AVG fighter had just been force-landed with an overheated engine caused by bullet damage, and it was abandoned by its pilot, First Squadron CO and ace Bob Sandell, in the nick of time. Lt Yamamoto received a posthumous individual citation for this deed.

The 50th claimed eight victories and four probables without loss. The AVG actually lost one Hawk 81-A-2 in air combat and Sandell's machine on the ground, whilst one Hurricane was also damaged. The AVG pilots claimed six kills and one probable in return.

Another sweep of Mingaladon was made by the 77th on 29 January, 20 Ki-27s being led by the Sentai CO, Maj Hirose. Hawk 81-A-2s and Hurricanes were again engaged, the 3rd Chutai

The remains of a Ki-27 from the 77th Sentai at Mingaladon airfield on 29 January 1942, the wounded pilot of the aircraft having crashed his machine deliberately in an attempt to destroy a Blenheim IV bomber that was parked nearby. The Ki-27 had been hit by Hurricanes of No 135 Sqn. Some sources identify the pilot as Sgt Maj Nagashima, but this is not certain. The Ki-27's demise was credited to Australian Plt Off W J Storey. The previous day Lt Kanecki Yamamoto from the same unit had crashed his Ki-27 into the parked AVG Hawk 81-A-2 of Bob Sandell, CO of the First Squadron (*James F Lansdale*)

diving on a formation of climbing AVG fighters. Its pilots claimed five kills, with two being credited to Lt Kuwabara. Lt Shizusada Nakao of the 1st Chutai also claimed a probable.

Two Hawk 81-A-2s had split off from the main formation moments prior to it being attacked, so the 'bouncers' were in turn 'bounced'. The 77th lost four Ki-27s, with Sgt Maj Nagashima being shot down by future No 135 Sqn Hurricane ace Plt Off W J Storey over the airfield and WO Yoshida, Sgt Maj Kanda and Sgt Kojima all failing to return

As JAAF units began to come under attack on their Thai airfields from AVG and RAF aircraft, many JAAF machines, like this Ki-27 from the 77th Sentai, were hastily camouflaged with a disruptive pattern applied to the upper wings and tailplanes only. This image reveals the tailwheel trolley used by groundcrews to manhandle aircraft into revetments (*James F Lansdale*)

from the mission. One of the stricken Ki-27s (whose pilot remains unidentified) made a failed jibaku dive on a Blenheim IV parked in a blast pen. The AVG claimed 12 kills and the Hurricane pilots (Storey and his CO, ace Sqn Ldr Frank Carey) two. There were no losses to the Allied units involved, although one Hawk 81-A-2 landed with battle damage.

The 'aerial exterminating action' continued into February, by which time additional Hurricanes had arrived in Burma and the fighting had become more attrition than extermination. The victory claims being made by both sides were overly optimistic, probably due to confusion in the air and the evasive diving away of attacked or damaged aircraft, rather than through any deliberate falsification, although propaganda also played a part. Throughout the month the Ki-27 units alternated fighter sweeps with bomber escorts as they attempted to destroy Allied air power in Burma.

On 4 February 13 Ki-27s of the 77th escorted 17 Ki-30s of the 31st Sentai in an uncontested raid on Toungoo. Two days later 25 Ki-27s of the 50th and 77th Sentais conducted a fighter sweep over Rangoon, again meeting eight Hawk 81-A-2s and six Hurricanes. Lt Kuwabara claimed one victory, as did Lt Beppu. The latter pilot, and WO Fujinaga, also got a probable each. Lt Kitamura was lost, however, possibly falling victim to Plt Off Storey. He recalled that two Ki-27s 'came down on my tail, so I again did a violent downward spiral then pushed the throttle through the gate and swept up into the sun, came down on the same two [Ki-27s] and carried out a quarter attack on the rearmost. After two bursts it spun down to the right, crashing east of Zayatkwin'. Maj Hirose's Ki-27 was also damaged in the fight, and he had to force land at Moulmein.

The 50th Sentai claimed three victories and four probables, although no Allied fighters were lost. Two pilots were wounded, however, and at least three aircraft received various degrees of damage. The AVG pilots claimed no fewer than seven 'I-97s', whilst their counterparts in Hurricanes claimed three. The American and RAF pilots, if optimistic about their claims, were by now at least gaining experience in countering the manoeuvrability of the Ki-27.

Twenty-two Ki-27s were despatched on a sweep by the 50th and 77th Sentais on 5 February. Lt Beppu of the latter unit, who by this time had claimed four destroyed and two probables over Burma, was shot down and killed during this engagement. Lt Nakao also had to land his damaged Ki-27 at Moulmein. Capt Eto and Lt Ogata claimed one victory each, whilst Lt Kuwabara and Sgt Niino were credited with single probables. 50th Sentai pilots claimed two destroyed and a probable for no loss, but again no Allied fighters had actually been downed.

On 21 February 23 Ki-27s, escorting 12 Ki-21s of the 31st Sentai towards Rangoon, ran into five Hawk 81-A-2s that were in turn escorting four Blenheim IVs of No 45 Sqn targeting Japanese Army columns at Kawbein. During the ensuing combat Lt Kuwabara claimed a Curtiss fighter destroyed, whilst Lt Ogata and WO Masao Hideshima were each credited with a probable. Several of the AVG fighters were damaged but none were lost, and the American pilots in turn claimed four Ki-27s destroyed and three probables – only one Japanese fighter was slightly damaged.

Four days later 23 Ki-27s of the 77th Sentai and 21 fighters from the 50th Sentai conducted another sweep over Mingaladon, this time accompanied by three Ki-44s of the 47th Independent Flying Chutai (see *Aircraft of the Aces 100* for further details). The pilots from the 50th and 77th claimed no fewer than 14 aircraft destroyed and seven probables, despite only three Hawk 81-A-2s actually being engaged – none were in fact shot down. Capt Eto claimed one destroyed and one probable, whilst Lt Kuwabara added another kill to his score. The AVG claimed four Ki-27s shot down, although none were in fact lost.

Moulmein was strafed by RAF and AVG fighters during the morning of 26 February, and that afternoon the 50th and 77th escorted another raid against Mingaladon, meeting Hurricanes and Hawk 81-A-2s over the airfield. Three Allied fighters were claimed by the 77th, credited to Lts Kuwabara, Kawada and Matsuo, with one probable claimed by Lt Shimoda. Although none were actually shot down, Flt Lt M C C 'Bush' Cotton's No 17 Sqn fighter was hit about 130 times when he winged over to dive on a Ki-27 leading the top cover. This was possibly the aircraft flown by Lt Kuwabara, which flicked up on its tail in a remarkable display of aerobatics and fired a very accurate burst through the port side of Cotton's fuselage, wounding him in the leg. He was able to get down safely, but the Hurricane was written off as beyond repair and destroyed with a hand grenade. During this fight the 50th claimed four Allied fighters shot down and two probables.

Sqn Ldr Barry Sutton, a Hurricane ace with Nos 135 and 136 Sqns during the defence of Burma, fought Ki-27s in 1942. He had occasion to recall a scornful pre-war newspaper article that had trumpeted the inability of the Japanese pilots to perform aerobatics;

'Many times since I have thought I would have liked to cram the man who wrote that article into the cockpit of my Hurricane as I twisted and turned, trying to dodge the front end of those slippery little "97s" as they clawed themselves around incredibly tight corners at a couple of hundred miles an hour.'

By the beginning of March the 77th Sentai had 24 Ki-27s serviceable, with a further ten aircraft requiring maintenance, whilst the 50th had only 18 serviceable examples and six requiring maintenance.

The 77th sent six of its Ki-27s on a sweep over the airfields around Rangoon on 6 March, where they were challenged by Hurricanes from No 17 Sqn. The Shotais of Capt Eto and Lt Nakajima each claimed a Hurricane shot down, one of these being credited to WO Saburo Hagiwara moments before his Ki-27 was badly damaged by Flg Off Lloyd Thomas. Hagiwara subsequently crash-landed at Kyaito, and returned to his unit the next day. While this fight was in progress, Lt Nagoshi's Shotai went down and strafed Mingaladon airfield, setting a Hurricane on fire and damaging another beyond repair.

After the fall of Rangoon on 9 March, the JAAF's fighter units began concentrating on the captured airfields around the capital as they were cleared and repaired. The 77th moved 15 Ki-27s into Hmawbe ('Highland Queen'), whilst the 50th, with 13 Ki-27s, took over Mingaladon. The 12th Hikodan – consisting of 29 Ki-27s from the 1st and 11th Sentais – was gradually transferred into Burma from Sumatra during this period. The unit had been tasked with reinforcing JAAF assets in-theatre in the final stages of the aerial campaign to eliminate the remaining Allied aircraft, which had been concentrated at Magwe, in central Burma. The Sentais took up residence on the captured airfield at Hlegu ('Pilsener', which had been known to the RAF as Zayatkwin and is sometimes misreported in references as Pegu, which was a town further north), where 800 barrels of aviation fuel left behind by the RAF were put to good use.

The Allies, who by this time had been reduced to just 38 aircraft in Burma – 23 fighters and 15 bombers – struck back at this concentration of air power as best they could. On 21 March a Shotai of Ki-27s from the 2nd Chutai of the 77th Sentai was on CAP at 11,500 ft over Maubin and Mingaladon when it intercepted a force of nine Blenheim IVs from No 45 Sqn on their way to attack the airfield. The bombers were unescorted, having earlier failed to rendezvous with their ten No 17 Sqn Hurricane escorts. Ki-27 pilot WO Takeo Tagata spotted the Blenheims at a distance of 20 km;

'I immediately informed Lt Shinjirou Nagoshi [Shotai leader] and MSgt Akamatsu, who had not seen the enemy formation. I increased my speed and headed in the direction of the foe, followed by my pilots.'

The Blenheim IVs were flying at the same altitude as the Ki-27s, which could not climb much higher because of heavy cloud at 13,000 ft. Lt Nagoshi led the trio of fighters in to attack the second bomber at the edge of the formation, opening fire at 200 m. 'The rotating turrets of the British aeroplanes were shooting at us – all 18 guns', WO Tagata continued. 'I kept on firing until I saw the face of the enemy crews at about a dozen metres. We were diving at a steep angle at maximum speed [about 300 mph]. I knew I had scored some hits'. Tagata then turned away, climbed and came back to make another run on the formation of Blenheim IVs, noticing that one was now streaming white fuel vapour from a wing.

At that moment he saw Lt Nagoshi's Ki-27 bank away steeply in a dive and heard him say 'I'm hit' over the radio. Tagata took command of the flight and made a raised fist gesture to Akamatsu to signify his determination, before attacking again;

'Looking around, I saw three additional Type 97 fighters climb through the thick anti-aircraft fire thrown up from our bases. At this moment I scored another hit on a Blenheim, which instantly burst into flames.

'The remaining seven Blenheims dropped their bombs over Mingaladon airfield. Columns of fire rose from the airfield. I could see a number of our aeroplanes explode on the ground. Some fuel tanks burned fiercely.

'Actually, our Type 97 fighters were slower than the Blenheims and so, while flying at full throttle, I prayed that we would receive deliveries of the newer and faster Hayabusa fighters as soon as possible.

'With three additional fighters now in the air, led by my classmate Takada from Tachiarai Flying School, we chased after the enemy formation for five minutes and caught up with them. We were then flying some 500 m above them. I began my dive, followed by Akamatsu. Within

Tomoari Hasegawa, the respected 'Vigorous Lieutenant' of the 11th Sentai, photographed here at Hankow, China, in 1940, was a Nomonhan Ki-27 ace in his mid-thirties with 19 victories to his credit who fought over Malaya and Burma as the unit's executive officer in the Sentai Hombu flight. He was to claim a further three victories flying the Ki-43 over New Guinea, before being posted to a transport unit. Hasegawa survived the war (*Yasuho Izawa*)

seconds we scored another hit – a Blenheim went down belching a column of black smoke.

'About ten minutes had passed since I had first spotted our foes. We were now about 20 km from our base. We still wanted to engage the remaining Blenheims, but we gave up and returned to base, leaving the rest of the enemy bombers to my classmate's unit.'

The wounded Lt Nagoshi had, meanwhile, crashed whilst attempting to land. Pulled from the wreckage alive, he was found to have been badly wounded by the Blenheim IV's return fire and died shortly thereafter. Despite Tagata's optimistic tally of three probables, claimed jointly with Akamatsu, and one confirmed for Lt Nagoshi, all the bombers survived the encounter. Most had been damaged, with one sustaining 57 bullet hits, and a pilot and a gunner had also been wounded. The Blenheim IV gunners in turn claimed two Ki-27s shot down, with two probables and two damaged.

Later that same day, just before 1330 hrs, the JAAF struck at Magwe. Initially, a fighter sweep of 31 Ki-27s from the 12th Hikodan was sent in, followed by two waves of heavy bombers – 25 Ki-21s of the 98th Sentai and 27 Ki-21s of the 12th Sentai, escorted by Ki-43s from the 64th Sentai. Finally, the airfield was targeted by ten Ki-30s of the 31st Sentai, escorted by Ki-27s of the 77th Sentai. Six Hurricanes and three Hawk 81-A-2s got off the ground, variously engaging the bombers and their escorts.

The Ki-27s of the 11th Sentai went after three Hurricanes from No 17 Sqn that attempted to intercept the bombers, claiming all three RAF fighters destroyed. Plt Offs K G Hemingway and A N Brooks were both hit and had to force land, whilst Plt Off H J Everard had to dive away after only one run at the bombers, as the Ki-27 escort fell on him 'like a swarm of angry bees'. As he pulled out of his escaping dive at low-level over Magwe, he spotted the 11th Sentai commander, Lt Col Tadashi Okabe, stooging along alone, and promptly shot him down at the end of the airfield. Okabe was the only casualty amongst the Ki-27 pilots.

Magwe was attacked again on 22 March, this time by 12 Kawasaki Ki-48 twin-engined light bombers of the 8th Sentai and 12 Ki-30s of the 31st Sentai, escorted by a large force of every available Ki-27 – the 12th Hikodan put up 34 fighters and the 50th and 77th 13 and 14, respectively. A second raid in the afternoon by 53 Ki-21s of the 12th and 98th Sentais brought about the final evacuation of the airfield, with the surviving Allied aircraft being withdrawn to Akyab, in northwest Burma, or into China. Flg Off C D C Dunsford-Wood of Westland Lysander II-equipped No 28 Sqn described the Ki-27s strafing Magwe with near impunity during the raid;

'A dozen 97s turning and twisting like birds behind one another as they shoot up the 'drome, their red suns and undercarriages clearly discernible, like toy *Frog* aeroplanes.'

The 'aerial exterminating action' had finally driven the Allied squadrons from their airfields and caused them serious losses, but it had not eliminated them entirely. The aerial campaigns over Burma and south China would continue.

FACING A NEW ENEMY IN CHINA

Although the Ki-27's operations in China after 7 December 1941 are poorly documented, it nevertheless continued to be operated as a frontline fighter in combat against the USAAF's nascent Fourteenth Air Force, whose pilots referred to it as the 'I-97'. The gradual build up of aircraft and preparation of airfields under the auspices of Gen Chennault did not go unobserved, and the Japanese, alerted to the possibility of China-based air raids against the Homeland, countered by reinforcing their air units in China.

The Imperial General Headquarters operational plan of 16 April 1942 stated as its objective that 'The primary mission will be to defeat the enemy in the Chekiang area and to destroy the air bases from which the enemy might conduct aerial raids on the Japanese Homeland'. The main responsibility for these operations fell to the 1st Hikodan, headquartered at Canton, in southeast China, which included the 10th DHC and the 54th Sentai. The unit had arrived in China via Formosa in November 1941, and then moved to Canton in February 1942.

Both Sentais were still equipped with the Ki-27, the 54th continuing to fly the Nakajima fighter in China until February 1943, whilst the 10th DHC began re-equipping with the Ki-43 in November 1942 when it transitioned into the 25th Sentai, with two Chutai, before expanding to three Chutai in the spring of 1943. The 25th would fight throughout the war in China, and it would include several Ki-43 aces within its ranks. These included seven-victory Nomonhan Ki-27 veteran Moritsugi Kanai, who would eventually become the unit's top scorer.

The 54th Sentai got off to a bad start in China, losing three aircraft and pilots to poor weather during the staging flight to Canton. One of those killed was the 1st Chutai leader, Capt Shoji Tomita. Then, on 25 April 1942, it flew a preliminary reconnaissance mission over Kweilin prior to joining the planned attacks against US airfields. During the mission Sgt Major Kazuka Kobayashi had to force-land his Ki-27 near Kweilin, and when the 2nd Chutai leader, Capt Toshio Dozono, attempted to land alongside the downed pilot in order to perform a Nomonhan-style rescue, he was quickly captured. One of these Ki-27s was later repaired and test flown by AVG personnel.

After its participation in the Burma campaign the 11th Sentai continued to attack US airfields in China from Mingaladon. On 5 May 1942 the Mitsubishi Ki-51-equipped 27th Sentai launched a strike against Paoshan, the light bombers being escorted by Ki-27s from the 11th Sentai and Ki-43s from the 64th Sentai. AVG P-40E pilots who intercepted the Japanese formation claimed seven shot down and three probables. Flight Leader Matt Kuykendahl of the First Squadron claimed one 'I-97' destroyed, whilst Second Squadron Leader 'Tex' Hill claimed a 'Zero' kill, Flight Leader Frank Schiel one unidentified fighter destroyed, Flight Leader John Bright an 'I-97' destroyed and one probable, Flight Leader Frank Lawlor two 'I-97s' destroyed, Freeman Ricketts one 'Zero' kill and one 'I-97' probable and Ray Hastey one fighter probable. All misidentified the single-engined, fixed-undercarriage Ki-51s of the 27th Sentai as 'I-97s' (Ki-27s).

The Japanese actually suffered five losses during the raid, comprising the three 11th Sentai Ki-27s of Sgt Majs Yoshio Sudo, Kan-ichi Suzuki and Nobuo Hiura and two Ki-51s from the 27th Sentai. The 11th claimed two of the P-40s destroyed, one of them providing Sgt Takeo Takahashi with his first victory. Both Schiel and Hastey failed to return following this engagement, the former having been forced down during the fight. After a three-day trek on foot, he managed to reach the AVG base at Yunnanyi, which was also home to a Chinese flying school. Hastey had run out of fuel and bailed out 40 miles from the airfield.

Sgt Takahashi went on to become one of the leading pilots of the 11th Sentai, flying the Ki-43 over New Guinea, where he claimed two F4Fs on 31 January 1943. Promoted to sergeant major, he joined the 52nd Sentai in April 1944 and participated in further air defence missions over Japan, flying the Ki-84 Hayate. In September 1944 the Sentai moved to the Philippines, where Sgt Maj Takahashi gained a reputation for fighting 'like a demon'. He continued to score, claiming two P-38s, one of which was shot down in full view of ground personnel, earning him promotion to warrant officer. By the time of Takahashi's death on 13 November 1944 (he was a passenger in a transport aircraft that was shot down over Manila Bay), he had claimed a total of 13 victories.

Eight Ki-27s from the 3rd Chutai of the 54th Sentai and five new Ki-45 Toryu ('Nick') twin-engined fighters from the re-equipped 84th Independent Chutai escorted five Ki-48s from the 90th Sentai that targeted Kweilin on 12 June. The formation was confronted by 11 Hawk 81-A-2s and P-40E Warhawks of the AVG's First Squadron, which had arrived at Kweilin the day before. The Curtiss machines had scrambled in response to the usual preliminary Japanese reconnaissance flight, and were staggered in three patrols – four fighters at 15,000 ft, four at 18,000 ft and three at 23,000 ft.

The Ki-27s were supposed to provide close escort to the bombers whilst the Ki-45s operated as fighter-bombers, carrying ordnance As it turned out, the AVG flight at 15,000 ft, led by ace Charlie Bond, attacked the lower of the two Japanese formations of twin-engined aircraft. The four fighters were able to make two passes at the Ki-45s before two of the Ki-27s intervened.

The 3rd Chutai leader Capt Yaichiro Hayashi was flying with a single wingman, and they raced to the aid of the Ki-45s as Bond made a third pass. Hayashi fired at his Hawk 81-A-2 and followed it down

A Ki-27 of the 54th Sentai shortly after its capture by Chinese troops at Kweilin, China, on 25 April 1942. The pilot of the fighter, Sgt Maj Kazuka Kobayashi, was obliged to force land with engine trouble whilst performing a reconnaissance sortie over the airfield. The 2nd Chutai leader, Capt Toshio Dozono, landed in an abortive attempt to effect a Nomonhan-style rescue, but he was immediately taken prisoner. It appears that Sgt Maj Kobayashi was killed shortly after he landed at Kweilin (*via Carl Molesworth*)

in a steep dive, claiming the fighter as destroyed. Bond, who had been hit by return fire (either from the Ki-45s or Ki-48s) crash-landed with a dead engine. Ace George Burgard, flying at 23,000 ft, saw a flight of four Ki-27s below him at 14,000 ft, so he dived on them. Having hit one of the fighters, he was then forced to break off his pursuit when he came under attack from another Ki-27. A third Ki-27 went after Peter Wright, setting his Hawk 81-A-2 on fire. Burgard then intervened, chasing the Ki-27 away and escorting Wright back to Kweilin. The latter overshot the runway when he attempted to land in his burning fighter, which flipped over. Wright survived with little more than a wrenched back, however.

Happy that his squadronmate was safe, Burgard then went looking for more JAAF aircraft with Lt Romney Masters. By then the Japanese fighter formations had broken up, and Burgard and Masters soon spotted Sgt Kunihiro Nakano of the 54th, flying in company with a Ki-45. Nakano evaded Burgard's first pass and then went after the Hawk 81-A-2 as it made a run on the Ki-45. Nakano fired and hit Burgard's left aileron, before diving away. The American followed him, firing a long deflection burst at the Ki-27. Nakano's aircraft skidded and fell off on one wing, hitting a mountain peak and exploding.

The 54th Sentai claimed three AVG fighters destroyed and two probables for the loss of Nakano. The 84th Chutai claimed two destroyed and two probables for the loss of two fighters.

In response to an AVG strafing attack against river shipping on the morning of 22 June, the 54th sent two Chutais of Ki-27s towards Hengyang that afternoon. The airfield was alerted by the warning net and six fighters of the 1st, 2nd and 3rd AVG squadrons, led by Ed Rector, managed to climb to 20,000 ft before the 14 Ki-27s arrived over Hengyang at 8000 ft. The American pilots claimed four destroyed and three probables, with one of the victorious pilots being Spanish Civil War veteran Capt Ajax Baumler – this was his first claim over China. Only 1Lt Mitsunori Akiyama was lost during the fight, however, the pilot attempting to crash his fatally damaged fighter onto Hengyang airfield in another jibaku dive. Three Ki-27s were damaged, with one being so seriously shot up that its pilot had to force land during the return flight to Hangchow.

Sgt Maj Kobayashi's Ki-27 was repainted in Chinese colours and insignia and examined with interest by AVG personnel (*Author collection*)

On 4 July the JAAF launched another attack on Hengyang, and this time the bombers were followed over the airfield by 12 strafing Ki-27s of the 54th Sentai. The fighters dived on two AVG machines encountered over the airfield, but they were in turn attacked by four more P-40Es that had climbed above them. The AVG pilots claimed four Ki-27s shot down, three probables and one damaged. 1Lt Keiji Fujino and Sgt Yoshio Yamada of the 54th were both killed and several other Ki-27s damaged. No P-40Es were lost.

During these three combats the 54th had claimed three AVG fighters shot down and two probables, but at a cost of five aircraft destroyed and three pilots killed. With nine pilots lost (including two Chutai leaders) over south China since February, demoralised 54th Sentai commander Maj Yasunari Shimada requested that his unit be transferred back to Japan to be re-equipped with the Ki-43.

A JAAF staff officer noted at the time that conducting surprise attacks was proving to be very difficult because of the enemy's precise aircraft observation and reporting network. The Ki-27 was also too slow to effectively confront the improved P-40E, its agility being effectively countered by the American hit and run tactics. 'The speed and firepower of the American fighters is formidable, and each time after striking and returning, they cannot be caught by the 97-Sen. Our pilots have to fire at fleeting targets'.

In September 1942 the 54th Sentai was withdrawn from China and transferred to the far north of Japan, remaining there on air defence duties until early 1945. It would retain the Ki-27 until February 1943. The Fourteenth Air Force would continue to encounter Ki-27s in combat over China, however – at Canton on 27 November 1942, and as late as 16 August 1943 when two Warhawks of the 76th FS on a reconnaissance mission over Hankow were unsuccessfully challenged by a pair of 'Nates' near Yochow.

A head-on view of the captured Ki-27, showing the fighter's elegant lines and relatively long wingspan (*Author collection*)

CONSOLIDATION AND DEFENCE

As the fighter Sentais gradually re-equipped with the Ki-43 and Ki-44 during 1942-43, the Ki-27 was destined to soldier on as ancillary equipment and also fulfil an essential secondary function as a fighter trainer. Many of the young men entering flying training had grown up inspired by the deeds of the famous aces flying the 97-Sen over Nomonhan, avidly devouring the newspaper and bulletin board accounts of the fighting. Three to four years later they found themselves in the cockpit of the same aircraft, learning to become fighter pilots themselves.

Those fighter Sentai in garrison and air defence roles away from the main fronts continued to use the Ki-27 as mainline equipment. For example, the 26th Sentai, deployed in the Philippines, retained the aircraft as principal equipment until September 1943. The 9th Sentai and the Kyodo Hiko 204th Sentai (an operational training unit) converted from the Ki-27 to the Ki-43 in May 1943 on airfields in Manchuria.

It was remarkable that a fixed undercarriage fighter with an armament configuration that had been standard in World War 1 should have been expected to soldier on well into the Pacific War.

Ki-27 versus B-25

In November 1941 Premier Hideki Tojo had prioritised aircraft resources to the invasion forces about to embark on securing Japan's territorial ambitions. The reduced number of fighters available for Homeland air defence was deemed to be adequate to defend Japan from retaliatory attacks in the first months of hostilities.

At the time of the Doolittle Raid on Japan on 18 April 1942 (see Osprey *Campaign 156* for further details), the Ki-27 was still the principal air defence fighter in Japan, equipping the 5th Sentai at Kashiwa and Matsudo and the 244th Sentai at Chofu. These two units were entrusted with the protection of the Kanto sector within the Eastern District, which was considered to be of special importance because of its governmental and industrial infrastructure, its rice production and the presence of the Imperial Palace in Tokyo.

The 244th Sentai was reported to have a strength of 19 Ki-27s in two Chutais. The 5th Sentai also had two Chutais equipped with around 25 Ki-27s, and

The 102nd DHC was established as a 'secret' Home Defence interceptor unit at Akeno in July 1941, becoming the third Chutai of the 13th Sentai in November of the same year. The Ki-27 was the only fighter type available to defend Japan at the outbreak of the Pacific War, with just 93 aircraft in four Sentai, plus 25 examples on Formosa, protecting the home islands. These fighters were photographed at Akeno during the summer of 1941 as the unit worked up. The white 'bandages' behind the Hinomaru signify Home Defence operations (*Hiroshi Sekiguchi via Yasuho Izawa*)

These brand new Ki-27 Otsu fighters have been gathered together for an 'Aikoku' or Patriotism presentation ceremony to dedicate aircraft funded by public or private subscription. Machines acquired this way were marked with a dedication number and legend on the fuselage just forward of the tail, as seen here (*Author collection*)

these machines provided an ancillary fighter training role as well as air defence. In the Central District at Kakogawa, the 13th Sentai, with three Chutais and about 37 Ki-27s, performed a similar function to the 5th, undertaking both training and air defence, as did the 4th Sentai at Tachiariai in the Western District with two Chutais and 25 Ki-27s. The 13th Sentai had incorporated the 102nd Dokuritsu Hiko Chutai (a special interception unit at the Akeno Flying School) as its 3rd Chutai in July 1941.

All of these units were part of an air defence system with very limited radar capability that relied primarily on observer stations on land using the telephone network and picket boats at sea using radio for early warning. It was all the more surprising, therefore, that the air defence units were able to intercept a number of the Doolittle Raiders, albeit with little success.

On 18 April, when Ichiro Hasegawa heard the air raid siren sounding in the factory in which he worked in Kamata, Tokyo, he took shelter, but his curiosity kept his eyes on the sky. He watched a B-25 approach at low level, followed by a single Ki-27. The fighter initially dived to gain speed, before pulling up to fire at the bomber;

'Suddenly, white smoke extended from the B-25 to the tailing Ki-27. For a moment it looked as though the two aeroplanes were bridged with a wide white belt, which enveloped the Ki-27.'

The fighter was being flown by Lt Yasuhide Baba of the 5th Sentai, who would only claim damage to the B-25 he had attacked – 40-2303 *Whirling Dervish*, flown by 1Lt Harold F Watson. TSgt Eldred V Scott, engineer/gunner in the B-25, engaged Baba's Ki-27;

'Tracers were looping up at us from behind and below from a single fighter that was only 100 yards away from us, and pointing straight at me! I opened fire, only to find that my gunsight had fogged up. All I could do was keep my finger on the trigger and aim with tracers. As my bullets came closer and closer, the enemy fighter fell off on its left wing and I never saw it again. I think I got him, but I'll never be able to swear to it.'

Lt Baba survived the encounter to later command the 5th Sentai's 1st Chutai, and eventually the Sentai, flying the Ki-100 in the closing stages of the war. The smoke seen by Ichiro Hasegawa was probably from Lt Baba's guns, as the Type 89 kai 7.7 mm machine guns fitted in the Ki-27 fired a type of incendiary ammunition that left a conspicuous smoke trail. The preferred ammunition mix in the Ki-27 was a matter for each individual unit, the 64th Sentai, for example, using a combination of one tracer to one incendiary to two armour piercing rounds in every four links.

Of the 34 air defence pilots who intercepted the raiders in the Tokyo area on 18 April 1942, only three were able to claim damage to the enemy bombers, and no B-25s were shot down.

Ki-27 versus B-29 – Japan

In response to the Doolittle Raid, immediate action was taken to increase and improve Homeland defence fighter capability. Even so, the 244th Sentai would not finally relinquish its Ki-27s for new Ki-61 Hien ('Tony') fighters until July 1943. The 4th Sentai at Ozuki, in western Honshu, began re-equipping with the twin-engined Ki-45 Toryu ('Nick') fighter in early 1943, but retained a number of Ki-27s as secondary equipment. Even by late 1944, the 4th was still operating the obsolete aircraft to provide fighter training to cadet pilots assigned to the unit.

At about that time, in response to recent B-29 raids on targets in Kyushu, the 4th decided to sortie the Ki-27s in actual air defence missions. The 15 Ki-27 fighters in the unit were organised as a 4th Chutai, with seven cadet pilots and seven more experienced NCO pilots all being led by Lt Fujisaki.

For air defence missions the obsolete Ki-27s would receive normal fuel, rather than the alcohol adulterated, so-called 'A-Go' fuel used for training missions that was both despised and feared by the cadets due to its poor re-starting qualities in the event of an in-flight engine stall. Some of the cadet pilots expressed misgivings at the prospect of flying against the B-29 in the Ki-27 but they were admonished by their seniors, who told them that it was a fighter pilot's duty to make war with the equipment given to him. The Ki-27 might have been outdated and poorly armed, but even a 7.7 mm bullet could kill a pilot, so the cadets were told to aim at the cockpit of the B-29! They were urged to demonstrate their ability by achieving total control of their aircraft and exploiting it to the full.

After first participating in a B-29 interception on 19 December 1944 as observers in the rear gunner positions of the unit's Ki-45s, the cadet pilots finally sortied in their Ki-27s in reaction to a 40-bomber raid against Omura, on Kyushu, on 6 January 1945. The seventh and eighth Ki-27s in the takeoff sequence were flown by cadet pilot Ryuji Nagatsuka and his wingman Sgt Tanizaki. After takeoff, the aircraft formed up by circling at 3000 ft, before climbing towards the west. A B-29 formation that was already under attack by Ki-45s from the 4th Sentai was spotted between 13,000-14,500 ft, but the Ki-27 formation continued climbing to

This Ki-27 Otsu of the 2nd Chutai, 244th Sentai nosed over shortly after landing at Chofu, in Japan. The 244th was first formed as the 144th Sentai in July 1941 with two Ki-27-equipped Chutais that were charged with performing Home Defence duties for the Kanto area of Honshu – including the Imperial Palace in Tokyo, for which a Shotai of Ki-44s was said to be assigned. In April 1942 it became the 244th Sentai, and expanded to three Chutais in December of that year. The unit continued to fly Ki-27s until July 1943. The 244th was to become famous as a Ki-61 'Tony' Sentai, using the Kawasaki fighter to oppose B-29 raids on Japan. Thanks to its success in this role, the 244th became known as the 'Imperial Guards' or 'Tsubakudo' unit (*Picarella Collection*)

This well maintained Ki-27 Ko fighter from an unknown training unit in Japan had had its wheel fairings removed. It also has flare projectors fitted to the starboard wing flap (*Summer*)

16,000 ft. Lt Fujisaki then waggled his wings to signal that his pilots were to break up into pairs and conduct their attacks. Nagatsuka dived through cloud and emerged to see a B-29 about 1300 ft below him, flying towards the northeast;

'I dived. At a distance of 900 ft two upper turrets on the [Super]fortress opened fire. Tanizaki dived towards the bomber's tail, trying to eliminate the rear gun to assist my attack. As I had foreseen, the rear upper turret began launching 12.7 mm "ice-candies" at Tanizaki's aircraft. I took advantage of this to make a determined approach. At 650 ft I opened fire with a burst from both of my 7.7 mm guns to adjust my aim, then launched my own "ice-candies" at the B-29's nose. I was aiming at the pilot. Magnificent fireworks, but my cockpit was riddled with bullet holes. To evade the bomber's fire I had to go into a rapid sideslip, and this spoiled my aim. My bullets spent themselves in the void.

'Just as I was about to get clear with a tight zoom climb, I caught a glimpse of two motionless figures in the cockpit of the bomber – they looked like dummies, and their calm air incited me to fury. Tanizaki, before re-joining me, let off his "ice-candies" at the nose of the enemy aircraft. By the time we had regained our attacking altitude, the B-29 was already too far away. I must confess I was astounded at the speed of the Superfortress. Our Ki-27s were like gadflies on the back of a large, impassive cow. One flick of her tail and the gadflies scattered.'

Two newly delivered Ki-27 Otsu fighters at an unknown location. When fresh, the factory-applied paint, to the JAAF No 1 paint standard colour for 'Hairyokushoku' (ash-green colour), was quite bright and glossy, but with oxidisation and sunlight it soon degraded to a dull blueish grey in service (*Summer*)

Nagatsuka made two more attacks against B-29s in the following bomber formations, but again he had to sideslip to avoid their defensive fire. Out of ammunition, he signalled with the back of his hand to Tanizaki that he was returning to base, but the sergeant shook his head and the two Ki-27s then climbed to 16,250 ft, where they spotted a single, possibly damaged, B-29 heading west. Tanizaki dived and fired, hitting the bomber's fuselage and wings, but it flew on, seemingly impervious to the fire. Climbing back to join Nagatsuka, Tanizaki signalled that he too was now also out of ammunition, and the two frustrated pilots headed home. That evening Nagatsuka wrote in his diary;

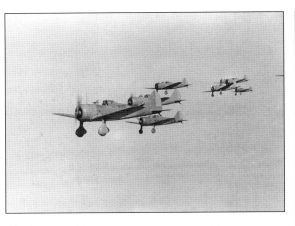

A formation of Manchukuo Ki-27s in flight. Although the Manchukuoan Air Force had been provided with more modern fighters, the Ki-27 was still flown against the B-29, with at least one aircraft credited with a ramming kill (*Kikuchi Collection*)

'First air battle. Result – nil. I realise now how difficult it is to fire accurately in the air. Our lack of training is indisputably against us. It is almost impossible to shoot down the Superforts with 7.7 mm bullets, but it would be cowardly to complain.'

Ki-27 versus B-29 – Manchukuo

As Manchukuo, Manchuria had been a vassal state effectively under Japanese control since February 1932, and the development of its military aviation had been strongly influenced by the air units of the Japanese Kwangtung Army. By the end of 1944, when the first B-29 incursions over Manchuria began, the Manshû Kokugun Hikotai (Manchukuo National Army Air Group) consisted of three operational Hikotai (Air Units), the 1st, 2nd and 3rd, each of which was approximately equivalent to a JAAF Sentai in terms of size, and an Independent Hikotai of approximately Chutai or squadron strength. It also maintained an Aviation School (Hikkô Gakkô) at Mukden with three Kyôdôtai (Training Units), as well as an Aviation Arsenal. Originally equipped almost wholly with the Ki-27, the Manchukuo fighter force had recently been augmented with additional Ki-43, Ki-44 and Ki-45 fighters, but many of these aircraft had no armament.

In response to the first B-29 raid against Mukden on 7 December 1944, the Aviation School scrambled its whole fighter force – 12 Ki-27s of the Takeshita unit, led by Maj Hirotoku Takeshita, 12 Ki-27s of the Shimada unit, led by Capt Shimada, three Ki-43 fighters flown by Capts Inoue and Hasegawa and 1Lt Nakaura, and a single Ki-44 flown by 2Lt Hayase. In addition, aircraft from the 2nd Hikotai, based at Mukden, were also scrambled. Two JAAF units based in Manchuria, the Ki-44-equipped 104th Sentai and the 21st Independent Air Squadron, flying the Ki-45, also participated in these interceptions (see also Osprey *Aircraft of the Aces 100* and Osprey *Aviation Elite Units 5* for further details). Maj Takeshita, who had taken off late because of gun problems with his Ki-27, was flying at 25,300 ft when he engaged a B-29 flying ahead and below him at 23,600 ft;

'When I opened fire at a range of about 1000 m [3300 ft], we were at roughly the same height. At full throttle my aircraft's engine was giving out its distinctive growl, and the whole machine was shaking. Under fire I pursued the enemy aircraft from Tie Xi to Bei Ling.

The pilot of a well-weathered Manchukuoan Air Force Ki-27 prepares for flight. This appears to be an ex-JAAF machine, where the Hinomaru insignia has been removed from the fuselage, leaving a patch of bare metal. It has the katakana character 'Ta' on the rudder, which might have been painted yellow. Manchukuo aircraft featured national insignia only on the wings. In the background, another Ki-27 carries a typical 'Gokoku' (Defence of the Fatherland) or presentation legend, indicating it was donated by the people of Mukden (*Kikuchi Collection*)

Suddenly, my aircraft was being tossed around like a leaf and anti-aircraft shells were exploding all around me, but harmlessly behind the intended target, the B-29. Fortunately, I did not fall victim to friendly fire.'

Later, Takeshita saw a B-29 drop out of formation and fall away, 'its silver wings reflecting the sun as it spun earthwards', with parachutes blossoming. It was probably *Humpin' Honey* (42-6299) of the 700th BS/462nd BG, flown by 1Lt Aurelius M Colby, which had been rammed by a Ki-44 of the 104th Sentai. Only two crewmen escaped by parachute. Approaching the parachutes, he saw one of his subordinates attacking the downed airmen, and intervened with hand signals to stop it.

After landing, Takeshita discovered that one of the Aviation School instructors, 1Lt Sonô Kasuga, also in a Ki-27, had attacked a B-29 from head on after it had turned north of Mukden and rammed it, killing himself. At first the 2nd Air Army HQ staff did not believe that the bomber had been brought down by ramming, but after the attack had been confirmed 1Lt Kasuga was acknowledged as having made the first taiatari (suicide ramming) attack by a Manchukuo aircraft, and he was posthumously promoted two ranks. The B-29 rammed and brought down by 1Lt Kasuga was possibly *Round Trip Ticket* (42-6262) of the 444th BG, flown by Maj Carl R Barnes. It had last been seen under attack by a Ki-45, and did not return to base. 1Lt Kasuga's ramming attack served as the inspiration to form a special unit – the Ranka Tokubetsu Kôgekitai (Orchid Special Attack Unit) – to conduct similar taiatari against the B-29s.

During the 7 December raid Shuichi Ito, flying another Aviation School Ki-27, managed to make a single attack against a B-29 from ahead and above the bomber. He was amazed by the amount of defensive fire put up by the bomber as it turned towards him, bringing both forward turrets to bear. After successfully breaking away, Ito found that he was unable to make another attack because of the speed and altitude difference between his Ki-27 and the B-29. Maj Takeshita also experienced these difficulties in trying to intercept a B-29 in a Ki-27;

85

'The service ceiling was up to 33,000 ft. On several occasions I climbed as high as that. The Ki-27 could reach 10,000 ft in just under three minutes, but making it up to 16,000 ft took another five. All told, reaching 26,000 ft would end up taking the best part of 30 minutes. At altitudes higher than that, you weren't able to mount a swift attack. When you performed a single attack, the aircraft ended up losing altitude, and in the meantime the enemy had put distance between you. Fortunately, there was time to regain altitude before the next enemy formation arrived, and you mounted the next attack.'

On the 21 December 1944 the B-29s raided Mukden for the second time, and again the Manchukuo fighters of the Aviation School, the 2nd Hikotai and the Orchid Special Attack Unit were scrambled to intercept. A total of 40 Superfortresses bombed the target, approaching in separate formations at three-minute intervals. 2Lt Morio Nishihara of the 2nd Hikotai, flying a Ki-27, was too low to attack the first formation of bombers, but having climbed to 25,300 ft, he deliberately rammed a B-29 in the fourth formation. His fighter struck one of the engines of *Ole Campaigner II* (42-24715), a 794th BS/468th BG aircraft flown by Capt Charles Benedict. After the impact the B-29's wing folded and the bomber plunged earthward, only the radio operator, SSgt Elbert Edwards, surviving by parachute descent. Nishihara's body fell from the Ki-27 during impact, his parachute deploying by lanyard, but he had been killed instantly.

SPECIAL ATTACKERS

Even these desperate attempts to intercept the B-29 did not spell the end of the operational use of the Ki-27. In late 1944 the Japanese military determined that special attacks would be the most effective way to destroy Allied surface fleets threatening invasion of the home islands. In pursuit of this doctrine they began to form special attack units (tokubetsu kôgeki tai, usually abbreviated to tokkôtai), and undertook the wholesale conversion and preparation of obsolete types of aircraft (including the Ki-27) with which to conduct the operations. The death knell of the Ki-27 was almost literal, as teenage student pilots flew the fighters, laden down with 250 kg and 500 kg bombs, in desperate one-way missions to sink Allied ships.

After becoming obsolete for frontline service, the Ki-27 continued to be used in operational training units and in special attack squadrons that flew the fighter in kamikaze attacks against Allied ships. Many of these units adorned their aircraft with brightly coloured, morale-boosting insignia, sometimes reflecting the unit designation. Here, a Ki-27 operational trainer believed to belong to the 117th Kyouiku Hiko Rentai (Training Flying Regiment) is being started up on an airfield (*Summer*)

APPENDICES

Ki-27 Aces

Name	Sentai/Chutai	Claims	Fate
Hiromichi Shinohara	11/1	58	KIA
Mitsuyoshi Tarui	1/1	38	KIA
Kenji Shimada	11/1	27	KIA
Shogo Saito	24/1	26+	KIA
Goro Furugori	11/3	25+	KIA
Tomio Hanada	11/3	25	AD
Zenzaburo Ohtsuka	11/3	22	KIA
Hitoshi Asano	1/2	22	SW
Bunji Yoshiyama	11/1	20	KIA
Saburo Kimura	11/3	19	KIA
Takeo Ishii	1/1	18	SW
Shoichi Suzuki	24/1	17	KIA
Mamoru Hanada	11/2	17	MW
Muneyoshi Motojima	1/1	16+	KIA
Hyoe Yonaga	24/2	16	SW
Riichi Ito	11/4	16	SW
Yoshihiko Yajima	1/2	16	KIA
Megumu Ono	1/2	15	AD
Koji Motomura	11/2	14	KIA
Tokuyasu Ishizuka	11/2	14*	SW
Jiro Okuda	11/4	14	KIA
Takaaki Minami	11/4	14	SW
Masao Ashida	11/3	13	KIA
Yutaka Aoyagi	11/1	12+	AD
Koichi Iwase	11/1	12	SW
Goro Nishihara	24/2	12	SW
Koji Ishizawa	24/2	11+**	SW
Eisaku Suzuki	11/1	11	KIA
Takayori Kodama	1/2	11	KIA
Tokuro Fukuda	11/4	11	SW
Taro Kobayashi	11/2	10	KIA
Daisuke Kambara	11/3	9+	SW
Shintaro Kashima	11/4	9+	KIA
Saiji Kani	24/1	9	KIA
Yutaka Kimura	24/1	9	SW
Akira Ina	11/2	9	SW
Hitoshi Tobita	1/2	8***	SW
Megumu Ono	1/2	7	AD

Notes

Sentai/Chutai at time of flying Ki-27

+ Plus one B-29

** Claims after December 1941 unknown

*** Includes one Vildebeest at Endau

Aces with Ki-27 Claims (in parentheses)

Name	Sentai/Chutai	Claims	Fate
Satoshi Anabuki	50/3	39 (3)	SW
Isamu Sasaki	50/3	38 (1+)	SW
Yasuhiko Kuroe	59	30 (2)	SW
Rikio Shibata	11/4	27 (14)	KIA
Moritsugu Kanai	11/1	26 (7)	SW
Isamu Hosono	1/HQ Shotai	26 (21)	KIA
Chiyoji Saito	24/2	24+ (21)	KIA
Tomoari Hasegawa	11/1	22 (19)	SW
Jozo Iwahashi	11/4	21+ (20)	KIA
Katsuaki Kira	24/2	21 (9)	SW
Naoharu Shiromoto	11/4 and 1/3	21 (17)	SW
Tateo Kato	64	21 (5)	KIA
Haruo Takagaki	11/2	17+ (15)	AD
Misao Inoue	1/2	16 (8)	AD
Toyoki Eto	77/1	15 (11 inc 4 probables and 1 shared)	SW
Toshio Sakagawa	11/2	15 (?)	AD
Toshio Matsuura	1/2	15 (10+)	AD
Masatoshi Masuzawa	1/2	15 (?)	SW**
Takeo Takahashi	11/3	13 (1)	KIA
Noburo Mune	50/3	14 (?)	KIA
Tadashi Shono	10 DHC	14 (?)	KIA
Yoshiro Kuwabara	77/3	13+ (12)	MIA
Shoji Kurono	24/2	13.5 (12)	SW
Katsutaro Takahashi	59/2	13+ (2)	KIA
Mitsugu Sawada	2nd Daitai/1 Chutai	12(3)	KIA
Eiji Seino	10 DHC	10+	SW
Iwataro Hazawa	10 DHC	10+ (?)	KIA
Kyushiro Ohtake	10 DHC	10+ (?)*	SW
Tokuya Sudo	64/2	10 (4+ inc 2 shared)	KIA
Miyoshi Shimamura	1/1	10 (9 inc 3 probables)	SW
Iori Sakai	64/2	9+ (4+)	SW
Yoshio Hirose	77	9 (3)	KIA
Takeshi Shimizu	64/1	9 (3 inc 1 probable)	SW
Yamato Takiyama	11/2	9 (7 inc 5 probables)	SW
Takeomi Hayashi	59/2	9 (2)	SW
Isamu Kashiide	59/2	9 (2)***	SW
Teizo Kanamaru	50/3	8 (3)	KIA
Masao Miyamaru	50/2	8 (1+)	KIA
Hiroshi Sekiguchi	64/1	7 (4)	SW

Notes

Sentai/Chutai at time of flying Ki-27 only
* Also claimed one F6F flying the Ki-79
** Died of his wounds post-war
*** Claimed 7 B-29s
KIA - Killed in Action
SW - Survived War
AD - Accidental Death
MW - Mortally wounded in action
MIA - Missing in Action

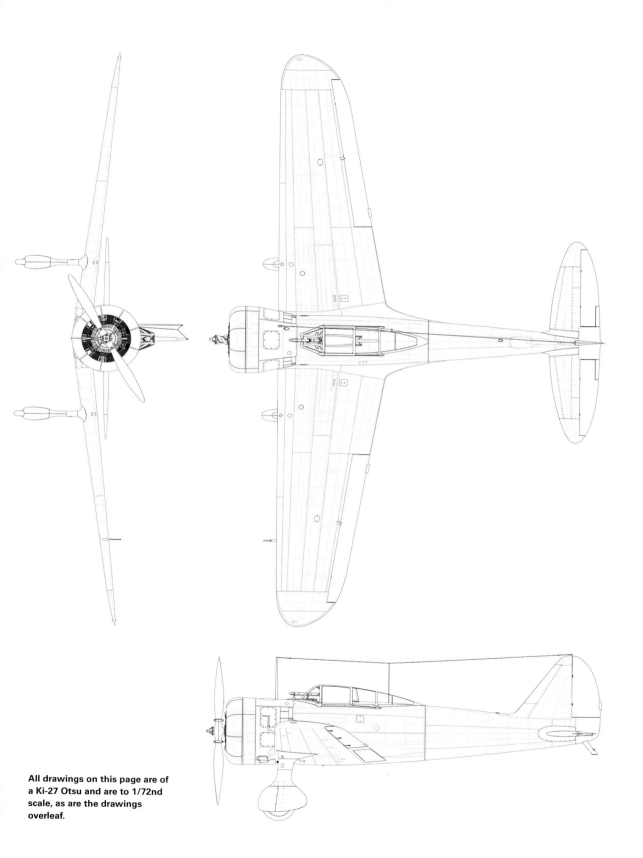

All drawings on this page are of
a Ki-27 Otsu and are to 1/72nd
scale, as are the drawings
overleaf.

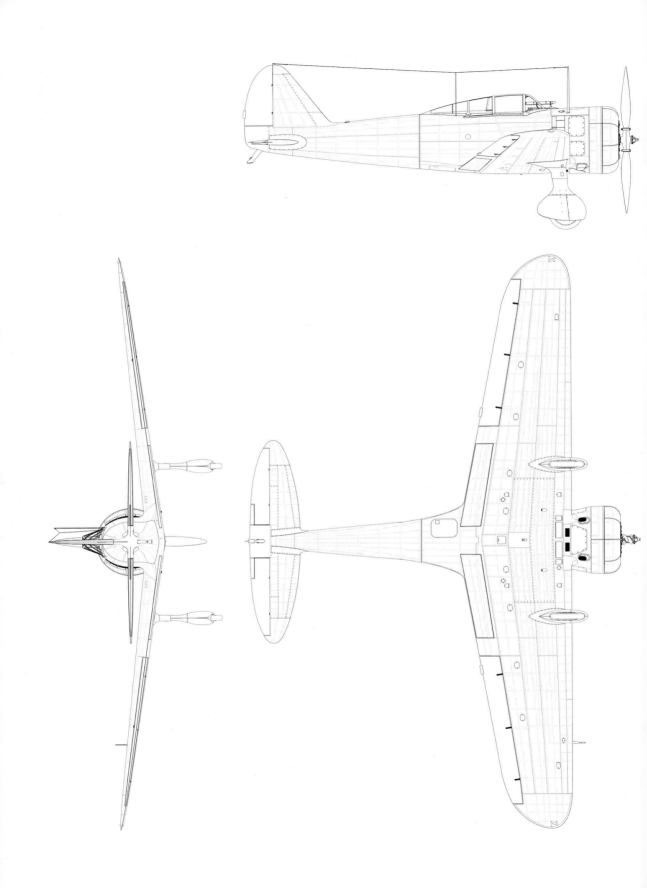

1

Ki-27 Otsu of Sgt Maj Goro Nishihara, 2nd Chutai, 24th Sentai, Nomonhan, summer 1939

Sgt Maj Nishihara flew this aircraft regularly during the Nomonhan campaign within 1Lt Hyoe Yonaga's flight in the 2nd Chutai. The stripes on the tail in the Chutai colour red symbolise '2' and '4' for the Sentai, whilst the blue katakana character 'Su' identifies the individual aircraft. The significance and colour – depicted here in black – of the dark fuselage stripe ahead of the white senchi hiyoshiki (war front sign) is unknown. Nishihara, an ace with 12 victory claims over Nomonhan, gained fame for his daring rescue of the Sentai commander, Lt Col Kojiro Matsumura, who had force landed during air combat on 4 August 1939.

2

Ki-27 Otsu of Sgt Maj Shogo Saito, 1st Chutai, 24th Sentai, Nomonhan, summer 1939

Sgt Maj Saito's Ki-27 – the subject of this volume's cover art – bears the Sentai tail insignia in white for the 1st Chutai. The colour of the stripe behind the senchi hiyoshiki is also unknown, but it is depicted here in blue. This aircraft does not appear to carry an individual katakana character on the tail. Sgt Maj Saito was the Sentai's most successful pilot during the Nomonhan campaign, claiming 25 victories.

3

Ki-27 Otsu of 1Lt Hyoe Yonaga, 2nd Chutai, 24th Sentai, Nomonhan, summer 1939

This Ki-27 was a presentation aircraft, bearing the patriotism number 318 on the rear fuselage. Flown by Sgt Maj Chiyoji Saito and Goro Nishihara, as well as 1Lt Yonaga, it shot down the most aircraft of all the Ki-27s in the Sentai. The katakana tail character is 'Mi' and the fuselage stripe to the rear of the senchi hiyoshiki was reported to be blue. The factory finish for the Ki-27 was overall JAAF paint colour No 1 Hai ryoku shoku (ash green colour), which was made from black, white and yellow oxide pigments. When new it was a bright, glossy grey-green, but once in service the paint gradually weathered to a dull dove grey or blueish grey.

4

Ki-27 Otsu of Capt Toshio Sakagawa, 3rd Chutai, 24th Sentai, Hailar, Manchuria, January 1940

Capt Sakagawa was the leader of the 3rd Chutai, and his aircraft was distinguished by a broad vertical fuselage stripe and diagonal stripes on the tailplanes. The distinguishing Chutai colour was yellow. He led the 3rd Chutai from September 1939 through to March 1940, participating in the last of the Nomonhan fighting during an attack against Tamsag-Bulak on 15 September 1939. The aircraft is depicted here fitted with a single range-extending auxiliary fuel tank under each wing and the lower wheel fairings removed – a common practice on wet and muddy landing fields.

5

Ki-27 Otsu of Capt Kenji Shimada, 1st Chutai, 11th Sentai, Nomonhan, summer 1939

The four-Chutai 11th Sentai, which followed the 24th into action, was the highest scoring Ki-27 unit at Nomonhan, and the 1st Chutai claimed the most victories. The Ki-27 of its commander, Kenji Shimada, who claimed 27 victories, is one of the better known aircraft of the conflict. Shimada's fighter sports the Sentai's lightning bolt device on the tail, in white for the 1st Chutai, a broad red fuselage band denoting his command status and eight Soviet victory stars. These were painted on the fuselage during the June lull in aerial action, and signify claims Shimada made in two days of air combat in May.

6

Ki-27 Otsu of WO Hiromichi Shinohara, 1st Chutai, 11th Sentai, Nomonhan, summer 1939

WO Shinohara was the highest scoring JAAF ace over Nomonhan, with claims for 58 victories. He flew in Capt Shimada's 1st Chutai, hence his similarly marked Ki-27. The ten Soviet victory stars on this machine were also applied during the June lull, and they denote kills claimed in two days of air combat in May. The significance of the red-painted cowling is unknown, as it was not seen on all aircraft within the Chutai. This marking possibly identified aircraft in Shimada's own flight. Shinohara was forced down over Soviet territory in this aircraft on 25 July, but he was rescued by Sgt Maj Koichi Iwase. Thereafter, Shinohara flew a different red-cowled Ki-27 marked with three vertical white fuselage stripes.

7

Ki-27 Otsu C/n 331 of Capt Jozo Iwahashi, 4th Chutai, 11th Sentai, Nomonhan, summer 1939

Capt Iwahashi commanded the 4th Chutai of the 11th Sentai throughout the Nomonhan conflict, claiming a total of 21 victories, including probables. He was awarded the Order of the Golden Kite (Kinshi Kunsho), 4th Grade, for his success.

8

Ki-27 Otsu C/n 5326 of Cpl Moritsugu Kanai, 1st Chutai, 11th Sentai, Nomonhan, summer 1939

Cpl Kanai was one of the youngest pilots in the 11th Sentai over Nomonhan, and he sometimes flew as WO Shinohara's wingman, claiming seven victories. The unusual red saltire on the fuselage of his presentation aircraft No 437 is based on a partial photograph, so it might not be a true representation of the actual design. During World War 2 Kanai became the 25th Sentai's top-scoring ace over China with a total of 26 victories. He survived the war to serve in the JSDAF as a major, changing his name to Hosaka. The veteran ace was killed in an accident in August 1972 whilst working as a flying instructor.

9

Ki-27 Otsu of C/n 345 Capt Koji Motomura, 2nd Chutai, 11th Sentai, Nomonhan, summer 1939

Capt Motomura commanded the 2nd Chutai of the 11th Sentai over Nomonhan, claiming 14 victories. His Ki-27 – another presentation aircraft, No 194 – sported distinctive red and white decoration on the wheel fairings and a broad red fuselage stripe. Motomura was killed in action near Usurouka airfield on 22 August 1939 after engaging a superior force of Soviet aircraft. Another presentation Ki-27, C/n 292 with an 'angry head' emblem purported to represent the Buddhist guardian deity Fu Dou Mei Ou, is said to have been flown by him at the time of his death but this seems unlikely as that aircraft fell within Soviet lines.

10

Ki-27 Otsu of Sgt Maj Yutaka Aoyagi, 1st Chutai, 11th Sentai, Wuchang, China, 1940

Sgt Maj Aoyagi had claimed ten victories over Nomonhan by the time he was wounded by tank fire on 25 July 1939 in a brave attempt to rescue WO Shinohara (see Profile 6). MSgt Koichi Iwase then landed under fire and rescued both Shinohara and Aoyagi. Aoyagi subsequently led a Shotai of the 11th Sentai during the invasion of Malaya and the East Indies, raising his total claims to at least 12 – the appearance of his Ki-27 during the Malayan campaign is unknown. The lightning bolt emblems on the undercarriage fairings of his Ki-27 are believed to have been a personal embellishment.

11

Ki-27 Otsu of Sgt Zenzaburo Ohtsuka, 3rd Chutai, 11th Sentai, Nomonhan, summer 1939

Sgt Ohtsuka became the second ranking ace of the 11th Sentai's 3rd Chutai over Nomonhan, claiming 22 victories. Although he survived the 1939 conflict to fly the Ki-27 during the Malayan campaign, Ohtsuka had not been credited with any further claims prior to being killed whilst attempting to take off during the B-17 raid on Kuantan airfield on 28 January 1942. His plain looking Ki-27, production number 370, displays the yellow lightning bolt of the 3rd Chutai, marked with the katakana character 'O' presumably for his surname.

12

Ki-27 Ko of Sgt Toshio Matsuura, 2nd Chutai, 1st Sentai, Nomonhan, summer 1939

Sgt Matsuura's Ki-27 was an older Ko variant, this version of the Ki-27 being distinguished by the solid rear canopy fairing with side windows. 1st Sentai aircraft were identified by the painted rudder and elevators, in red for the 2nd Chutai, with the Hiragana character for 'ma' identifying the pilot. The pattern of stripes on the fuselage is believed to identify the aircraft's Shotai, although this marking system has not been conclusively confirmed, and it was not continued throughout the conflict. Sgt Matsuura claimed ten kills over Nomonhan, and he was awarded the Order of the Golden Kite, 5th Grade, for rescuing his commanding officer following a battlefield landing. Matsuura continued to fly the Ki-27 over Malaya, the East Indies and Burma, as well as the Ki-43 over New Guinea, adding at least five more kills to his total.

13

Ki-27 Otsu of Sgt Maj Takeo Ishii, 1st Chutai, 1st Sentai, Nomonhan, summer 1939

Sgt Maj Ishii was one of the stalwarts of the 1st Chutai, claiming 18 victories against the Soviets. His Ki-27 was presentation aircraft 'Kitanihon Kisen (Northern Japan Liner) 307'. Such aircraft were purchased with patriotic subscriptions or donations, usually made by Japanese companies or collectives, and they were marked with the legend 'Aikoku' (love of country or patriotism) followed by the donating organisation and the number. Ishii's Ki-27 was, therefore, the 307th such aircraft purchased. The katakana character on the tail is 'wo'.

14

Ki-27 Otsu of Sgt Maj Mitsuyoshi Tarui, 1st Chutai, 1st Sentai, Nomonhan, summer 1939

Sgt Maj Tarui was the leading ace of the 1st Sentai and the second ranking JAAF ace over Nomonhan with 28 kills. He was also the third ranking JAAF ace of World War 2 with a total of 38 victories claimed, yet he is now little known outside Japan. After Nomonhan Tarui continued to fly the Ki-27 during the campaigns over Southeast Asia in 1941-42, and he went on to fly the Ki-61 with the 68th Sentai over New Guinea. Here, he was noted and admired for his calm, cheerful and courageous demeanour. When Tarui's unit was denuded of aircraft the personnel joined the ground fighting, and he was killed in a strafing attack on 18 August 1944. The exact meaning of the stripes on this aircraft are now unknown, but the red chevron probably indicates his leadership of the 2nd Shotai within the 1st Chutai. The katakana character on the tail reads 'fu'.

15

Ki-27 Ko C/n 91 of Sgt Maj Isamu Kashiide, 2nd Chutai, 59th Sentai, Nomonhan, September 1939

Sgt Maj Kashiide's Ki-27 displays the common practice of being flown with the sliding canopy removed to improve visibility. The unit's dramatic lightning flash insignia on the side of the aircraft has been depicted as red in previous artwork, the colour designating the 1st Chutai, but the Chutai colours assigned to the 59th are disputed. We have followed earlier references in depicting it here as dark blue, but it has also been described as black. The rudder is marked with the katakana character 'ka'. The 59th joined the fighting over Nomonhan very late in the campaign, and Kashiide only claimed two victories on 15 September. After subsequently graduating from the Army Air Academy with the rank of lieutenant, he went on to become a noted ace in the air defence of Japan against the B-29, claiming seven bombers shot down whilst flying the Ki-45 with the 4th Sentai. He was a Bukosho recipient and ended the war with the rank of captain.

16

Ki-27 Ko of Sgt Maj Katsutaro Takahashi, 2nd Chutai, 59th Sentai, Nomonhan, September 1939

Only the katakana character 'ta' on the rudder differentiates this machine, flown by Sgt Maj Takahashi, from the Ki-27 of Isamu Kashiide depicted in the previous profile. And like Kashiide, Takahashi also claimed two victories on 15 September 1939. After graduating from the Army Air Academy he became one of the leading aces of the 59th Sentai, flying the new Ki-43-I during the offensive over Malaya and the East Indies and claiming a further seven victories. Takahashi was killed on 14 December 1942 by strafing fighters during a scramble at Abis, on Timor, having been unable to reach his fighter before being struck down.

17

Ki-27 Ko of Maj Tateo Kato, 64th Sentai, Kwangtung, China, May 1941

This profile is partially speculative as it is based on a photograph of Maj Kato's Ki-27 that does not show the tail. The fuselage band might have been light blue, but is shown here as orange yellow, as recent research published in Japan suggests that its colour signified Kato's former command of the 1st Chutai, 2nd

Daitai whilst flying the Ki-10. The tail arrow is depicted here as white outlined in yellow, but it has also appeared in previous artwork as plain yellow. It might also have been white outlined in light blue, as this colour combination was subsequently used for Kato's command markings on his Ki-43-I. The three victory markings beneath the 64th's red eagle refer to claims made in support of an Army attack against Huizhou in May 1941, but they are not generally included in Kato's published victory listings. It was unusual for a frontline unit to still be using the Ko variant of the Ki-27 by mid 1941. Tateo Kato became an almost legendary figure in wartime Japan, being revered as 'Gunshin' Kato – 'War God' Kato. The leading JAAF ace over China during the period 1937-41, he was killed on 22 May 1942 by the gunner of an RAF Blenheim IV that he was pursuing near Akyab, in Burma. Kato had claimed 18 victories prior to his death.

18
Ki-27 Ko C/n 184 of 1Lt Iwori Sakai, 2nd Chutai, 64th Sentai, Ehrtaokou, China, November 1938
The arrow-headed flash on the nose of this aircraft was an early marking used by the 2nd Chutai from the autumn of 1938 through to the summer of 1939, but it was not applied to fighters during Nomonhan. The Sentai emblem was a red eagle painted beneath the cockpit (as seen on the previous profile). It has been asserted that the tail number on this fighter was also applied in red, but again we have chosen to follow earlier references, as there are clear differences in tone on the original photographs. Within the 2nd Chutai Lt Sakai was a renowned and skilled aviator who taught junior pilots in the unit flying and fighting skills that became known as the 'Sakai Method'. He later served as an instructor with the Akeno Flying School and as a test pilot for the Ki-61 and Ki-100 at the Army Aircraft Evaluation Centre, flying the Hien in the air defence role and claiming a B-29 shot down. Although Sakai claimed at least nine victories, some sources state that he scored as many as 15 kills.

19
Ki-27 Otsu of the 1st Chutai, 64th Sentai, Yuncheng, China, August 1939
This aircraft was probably flown by Sgt Maj Rinpei Tanaka, a veteran pilot of the 64th Sentai with at least five victories to his name. It is depicted here on the very eve of the unit's deployment to the Nomonhan conflict. The two white fuselage stripes indicate its assigned pilot's position of wingman in the 1st Shotai, the Shotaicho having a single broad stripe and the third wingman a single narrow stripe.

20
Ki-27 Otsu of Capt Iwori Sakai, 2nd Chutai, 64th Sentai, Canton, China, spring 1941
This aircraft, flown by the 2nd Chutai leader Capt Iwori Sakai, was photographed at Canton, in China, in March or April 1941. Recent references suggest that it was also flown by future ace 1Lt Yohei Hinoki, who was a Shotaicho in the 2nd Chutai and a protégé of Sakai, but he only joined the unit in June 1941 and scored his first victories over Malaya flying the Ki-43-I. By this time the 64th had adopted its famous arrow tail marking, this Ki-27 also having diagonal red and white stripes on the upper wing surfaces.

21
Ki-27 Otsu C/n 5001 of Lt Masao Okumura, 10th Dokuritsu Hiko Chutai, Canton, China, December 1941
Representative of the aircraft of this unit that participated in the attack on Hong Kong, this Ki-27 has been camouflaged in lustrous dark green paint but retains the red-painted spats that were the unit identification marking. Several pilots that participated in the attack were to subsequently become notable aces over China, including Sgt Maj Iwataro Hazawa, who was credited with 15 victories but personally claimed 40 destroyed or damaged in air combat, and Sgts Kyushiro Ohtake with ten victories and Eiji Seino with 10+ victories.

22
Ki-27 Otsu of the Hombu Shotai, 77th Sentai, Thailand, December 1941
Where possible, the Sentai HQ or Hombu formed a Shotai, usually consisting of the commander, his executive officer or adjutant and experienced wingmen appointed from the other Chutai. This Ki-27 is possibly the aircraft of the 77th Sentai commander, Maj Yoshio Hirose, and it is distinguished by the cowling rim, broad fuselage stripe and horizontal tail stripes in the Sentai Hombu colour of cobalt blue. The wheel spats have been removed – a common practice when operating from forward landing grounds to prevent mud clogging the wheel axles and causing the aircraft to tip over.

23
Ki-27 Otsu of Capt Yoshiro Kuwabara, 3rd Chutai, 77th Sentai, Thailand, December 1941
Capt Kuwabara was the 3rd Chutai leader, and he claimed a total of 12 victories flying the Ki-27 to become the 77th Sentai's most successful pilot during the invasion of Burma. Although the camouflage colours applied to this aircraft are unknown, we have chosen to depict them as those officially specified for the Ki-27 by the JAAF – namely khaki, olive green and indigo. This aircraft carries auxiliary fuel tanks, which, although significantly extending the range of the Ki-27, were not popular as they had an adverse effect on the aircraft's performance.

24
Ki-27 Otsu of the 1st Chutai, 50th Sentai, Mingaladon, Burma, March 1942
This aircraft was probably flown by the 1st Chutai leader, Capt Masao Morikawa, who replaced Capt Fujio Sakaguchi after he had been killed in action the previous month. It was camouflaged with olive green paint following several successful AVG and RAF attacks against Japanese airfields. The 50th Sentai followed the practice of 'naming' each aircraft with a kanji character painted on the rudder, in this case 'longevity'. At this time the Hinomaru was not usually displayed on the fuselage by the JAAF, and it is believed that the 50th Sentai applied it as an integral part of the unit's lightning bolt insignia.

25
Ki-27 Otsu of the 1st Chutai, 11th Sentai, Burma, March 1942
The references for this profile were taken from film footage of the unit's Ki-27s as they began operating from Hlegu, in Burma. The significance of the red and yellow fuselage stripe is unknown. As part of the 12th Hikodan, the unit, together with the 1st Sentai, had flown Ki-27s throughout the invasions of Malaya and the East Indies, before participating in the final stages of the aerial campaign over Burma. The 11th Sentai's most successful Ki-27 pilot was 1Lt Yutaka Aoyagi, who claimed more than 12 victories.

26
Ki-27 Otsu of Capt Hyoe Yonaga, 2nd Chutai, 24th Sentai, the Philippines, December 1941

This camouflaged Ki-27 of the 2nd Chutai leader displays a very unusual presentation of the unit insignia, with five instead of the more usual four stripes on the rudder. It also has red and white diagonal stripes on the tailplanes. Capt Yonaga was a Nomonhan ace with 16 victories, and although he led the 2nd Chutai during the Philippines campaign and in south China in the summer of 1942, he made no further claims.

27
Ki-27 Otsu of the 1st Chutai, 54th Sentai, south China, spring 1942

When the 54th Sentai was deployed against the AVG and the nascent Fourteenth Air Force in south China during the first half of 1942, it quickly lost nine pilots, including two Chutai leaders. Following these losses, and a recognition that the Ki-27 was outclassed, Sentai commander Maj Yasunari Shimada requested that his unit be sent back to Japan to be re-equipped with the Ki-43. In September 1942 the unit was transferred to air defence duties in the far north of Japan, although it later served in the Philippines – as did its detached 1st Chutai as the 24th DHC, which also saw action in Sumatra. The 54th was one of the last JAAF units to fly the Ki-27 in frontline offensive combat against Allied aircraft. The Sentai emblem represents a folded paper crane Oritsuru, the unit sometimes being referred to as Oritsuru Butai.

28
Ki-27 Otsu of Sgt Maj Totaro Ito, 2nd Chutai, 5th Sentai, Kashiwa, Japan, April 1942

Sgt Maj Ito flew this Ki-27 on air defence duties in Japan at the time of the Doolittle Raid, prior to graduating from the Army Air Academy and returning to the 5th Sentai as an officer to fly the Ki-45 Toryu over the East Indies and New Guinea, where he became an ace. Ito claimed a total in excess of 13 victories (all bombers, including nine B-29s) and was awarded both a commanding officer's citation and the Bukosho for his exploits. He survived the war with the rank of captain as 3rd Chutai leader, having, unusually, spent the whole of his wartime service in the same Sentai.

29
Ki-27 Otsu of 2Lt Iichi Yamaguchi, 68th Shinbutai leader, Chiran, Kyushu, Japan, April 1945

Representative of the large numbers of obsolete Ki-27s deployed in specially formed Shinbutai (Shinbu [stirring the martial spirit] and tai [unit]) for the Tokubetsu kōgeki (special attack or suicide operations) against American warships sailing off Okinawa. This aircraft was flown by the Shinbutai leader, the characters of whose family name are painted on top of the fin and rudder. It is depicted here camouflaged in olive brown paint, although Shinbutai 'Nates' were also painted dark green, dark blue and dark grey for dawn and dusk operations. The 68th was formed by the Hitachi Air Training Division on 23rd March 1945 and established at Tenryu airfield in Shizuoka Prefecture, on Honshu, with a complement of 12 Ki-27s. The unit moved to Chiran, on Kyushu, and commenced operations on 8 April 1945 as part of the Dai Ni Kikusui Sakusen (2nd Floating Chrysanthemum Operation). Ki-27 'Nates' of this unit, armed with fixed 250 kg bombs, were responsible for severely damaging LCS(L) 57 and the destroyer escort USS Rall (DE-304) in suicide attacks on 12 April 1945.

30
Ki-27 Otsu of the Mukden Hikko Gakko, Manchukuoan Air Force, Manchuria, December 1944

Representative of the Ki-27s of the Mukden Aviation School, which sortied against B-29 raids in December 1944, this aircraft reveals evidence of a former Hinomaru stripped from the fuselage. It also carries the katakana character 'ta' on the rudder. Ki-27 pilots 1Lt Sono Kasuga and 2Lt Morio Nishihara of the Aviation School were credited with downing B-29s in fatal ramming attacks.

Plan Views and Back Cover
Ki-27 Otsu of Capt Shigetoshi Inoue, 1st Chutai, 1st Sentai, Saienjo, Manchuria, 1939

This aircraft is often associated with 21-victory Nomonhan ace Sgt Maj Isamu Hosono, who was photographed standing beside it, but in fact it was more usually flown by the 1st Chutai leader, Capt Shigetoshi Inoue. The chevron on the forward fuselage has been depicted as white in the past, but study of original photographs suggests that it might have been in the 1st Chutai colour of yellow. The katakana character on the rudder is 'Na'. Hosono often flew as third pilot to the Sentai commander, Lt Col Toshio Kato, in the Sentai Hombu Shotai. The significance of the colour and number of the various command and formation stripes on aircraft of this period has never been resolved.

BIBLIOGRAPHY

Axel, Albert and Kase, Hideaki, *Kamikaze – Japan's Suicide Gods*, Pearson Education, 2002
Bartsch, William H, *Doomed At The Start*, Texas A&M, 1992
Bartsch, William H, *Every Day A Nightmare*, Texas A&M, 2010
Chennault, Claire C, *Way of a Fighter*, Thorvardson & Sons, Tucson, 1991
Coox, Alvin D, *Nomonhan – Japan Against Russia, 1939*, Stanford University Press, 1985

Cotton, Sqn Ldr M C 'Bush', DFC OAM, *Hurricanes Over Burma*, Grub Street, 1995
Cull, Brian, with Sortenhaug, Paul and Haseldon, Mark, *Buffaloes Over Singapore*, Grub Street, 2003
Cull, Brian, with Sortenhaug, Paul, *Hurricanes Over Singapore*, Grub Street, 2004
Donahue, Flt Lt A G, DFC, *Last Flight from Singapore*, Macmillan, 1944

Dunn, Richard L, *Double Lucky? – The Campaigns of the 77th Hiko Sentai,* 2005

Eleftheriou, George and Domoto-Eleftheriou, Kiri, *The Eagles of Manchukuo 1932-1945,* Arawasi, 2009

Ford, Daniel, *Flying Tigers,* Smithsonian, Washington D.C., 1991

Gilchrist, Sir Andrew, *Malaya 1947 – The Fall of a Fighting Empire,* Robert Hale, London, 1992

Hata, Ikuhiko, Izawa, Yasuho and Shores, Christopher, *Japanese Army Air Force Fighter Units and Their Aces 1931-1945,* Grub Steet, London, 2002

Hemingway, Kenneth, *Wings Over Burma,* Quality Press, 1944

Hsu Long-hsuen and Chang Ming-kai, *History of the Sino-Japanese War (1937-1945),* Chung Wu, Taipei, 1971

Hsu Long-hsuen and Chang Ming-kai, *Air Operations of the Chinese Air Force in the Sino-Japanese War 1937-1945,* Chung Wu, Taipei, 1972

Ishikawa Shin, Dozone Katsuji and Miyako Minoru Cols, *Air Operation Record, Malaya, 1 st Period of Southeast Area operations,* First Demobilistion Bureau, Japan, 1946

Izawa, Dr Yasuho, *64th Flying Sentai,* Aero Album 1970 and 1971

Japan Defence Agency, *Army Air Operations in Southeast Asia,* Asagumo Shimbunsha, 1970

Japan Defence Agency, *Army Air Operations in China,* Asagumo Shimbunsha, 1974

Kotelnikov, Vladimir R, *Air War Over Khalkhin Gol,* SAM, 2010

Maslov, Mikhail, *Osprey Aircraft of the Aces 95 – Polikarpov I-15, I-16 and I-153 Aces,* Osprey, 2010

Miklesh, Robert C and Abe, Shorzoe, *Japanese Aircraft 1910 – 1941,* Putnam, London, 1990

Molesworth, Carl, *Sharks Over China,* Brassey's 1994

Nagatsuka, Ryuji, *I Was A Kamikaze,* MacMillan, 1974

Nakayama, Masahiro, *The Skies Over China,* Dai Nippon Kaiga, Tokyo 2007

Nedialkov, Dimitar, *In the Skies of Nomonhan,* Propeller Publishing, Sofia 2005

Nonaka, Col, *(CinC Operations, 3 rd Air Force), Southeast Area Operation Records, Phase II,* First Demobilisation Bureau, Japan, 1946

Olynyk, Frank, *Stars & Bars – A Tribute to the American Fighter Ace 1920-1973,* Grub Street, 1995

Ruffato, Luca, *Chronology of Air Operations During the Philippines Campaign, December 1941 to May 1942,* 2011

Sakaida, Henry, *Osprey Aircraft of the Aces 13 – Japanese Army Air Force Aces 1937-45,* Osprey, 1997

Shiba, Maj Takira and Others, *Air Operations in the China Area 1937-1945,* Japanese Monograph No 76, HQ USAFFE and 8th Army, Tokyo, 1956

Shiba, Maj Takira and Others, *Air Defence of the Homeland,* Japanese Monograph No 23, HQ USAFFE and 8th Army, Tokyo, 1956

Shores, Christopher, Cull, Brian and Izawa, Yasuho, *Bloody Shambles, Vols 1 and 2,* Grub Street, 1992 and 1993

Sutton, Wg Cdr Barry, DFC, *Jungle Pilot,* Macmillan, 1946

Takaki, Koji and Sakaida, Henry, *Osprey Aviation Elite Units 5 – B-29 Hunters of the JAAF,* Osprey, 2001

Unknown, *Army Type 97 Fighter (Famous Airplanes of the World No 29),* Bunrin-do, Japan 1991

Womack, Tom, *The Dutch Naval Air Force Against Japan,* McFarland, 2006

Yokoyama, Hisayuki, *Air Operational Leadership in the Southern Front,* Frank Cass, 2004

INDEX